MORE **WELSH** JOURNEYS

With best wishes

Jamie Owen

Published in 2006 by
Gomer Press, Llandysul, Ceredigion, SA44 4JL

ISBN 1 84323 738 5
ISBN-13 9781843237389
© text: Jamie Owen
© photographs of the journey: Martin Cavaney
© other photographs: individual
photographers as noted, namely
Dyfed Elis-Gruffydd, Aled Hughes,
Steve Lewis, Jeremy Moore, Hugh Olliff,
Jim Saunders, David Williams, Iolo Williams.

(photo right: Aled Hughes)

Design Concept MO-design.com

Printed in Wales at Gomer Press,
Llandysul, Ceredigion SA44 4JL
www.gomer.co.uk

MORE **WELSH** JOURNEYS

JAMIE OWEN

PHOTOGRAPHS OF THE JOURNEY BY MARTIN CAVANEY

Gomer

CONTENTS

36

102

76

56

122

10

INTRODUCTION

Welcome to my summer of travels around Wales. I spent much of 2006 wandering parts of the country that I previously didn't know terribly well, finding delightful nooks and crannies and magnificent landscapes. What I knew of these places from fleeting visits had persuaded me that it would be worth getting to know them more intimately. So on each of the six journeys I made during the spring and summer, my endeavour was not only to get under the skin of a place, but also to experiment with modes of travel – which often gave a completely new perspective.

I have sailed around Wales three times but until now never explored the coast east of Cardiff. I know the coast of Pembrokeshire well but its hills and inland villages are just as beguiling and the slow route on horseback was the best grandstand seat from which to explore. I wanted to meet the eccentrics who keep the little trains of Wales running on time – they have been responsible for keeping alive one of the iconic images of the country. And the Gower peninsula is one of those places that I'm ashamed to say I didn't know well until now, despite its status as an Area of Outstanding Natural Beauty. Exploring part of the border in north-east Wales was an introduction to the picturesque Ceiriog valley and the busy market town of Oswestry. Finally, the eco-journey from Machynlleth all the way to Penarth was thought-provoking and often moving.

The background to these travels was a wider world that suffered a sad summer of ongoing travel disruption because of the threat of terrorism. It's interesting to remember that tourism in Britain was actually born out of a war-torn Europe which caused the disruption of the Grand Tour, with travellers being redirected to destinations closer to home. This time we met so many people who were discovering Wales for the first time because of concerns surrounding blocked-up airports and worse.

At the time of writing, it's good to know that Wales has just enjoyed one of its most successful years in tourism. Faced with uncertainty regarding long-haul security and concerns about the environmental damage of air travel, visitors are coming to Wales in ever greater numbers. They discover a country that is stunningly beautiful, full of fascinating people and worthy of many happy returns.

Here you'll find my diaries, scribbled between breaks in filming, as we shot the documentaries for my series of 'Welsh Journeys' for BBC Wales. I was in the company of an intrepid crew who were good humoured and wonderful company for many weekends: our director Rob Finighan, cameramen Richard Longstaff and Tony O'Shaughnessy, sound recordist Dafydd Parry, and assistant producer Ann Summerhayes. Photographer Martin Cavaney joined us throughout the summer and took superb shots of our journeys.

Remember that these are simply the stories of my personal journeys – on horseback, sailing and cycling, as well as driving. Of course, you won't get a definitive history of any of these wonderful places from my musings. Nevertheless, I hope that from the comfort of your armchair you enjoy my journeys around Wales as much as I did. Better still, go and explore these parts for yourself – I hope this book might be inspiration!

Jamie Owen, 2006

TAL-Y-LLYN

MAGIC ON RAILS

Driving the engine is not unlike tending the Sunday joint in a roasting oven. But peering through the porthole at the track swaying rhythmically in front, I can see why these people are hooked. This is all-absorbing. The railway occupies every physical and mental resource you have and afterwards leaves you feeling you've done honest work that has left you exhausted but happy.

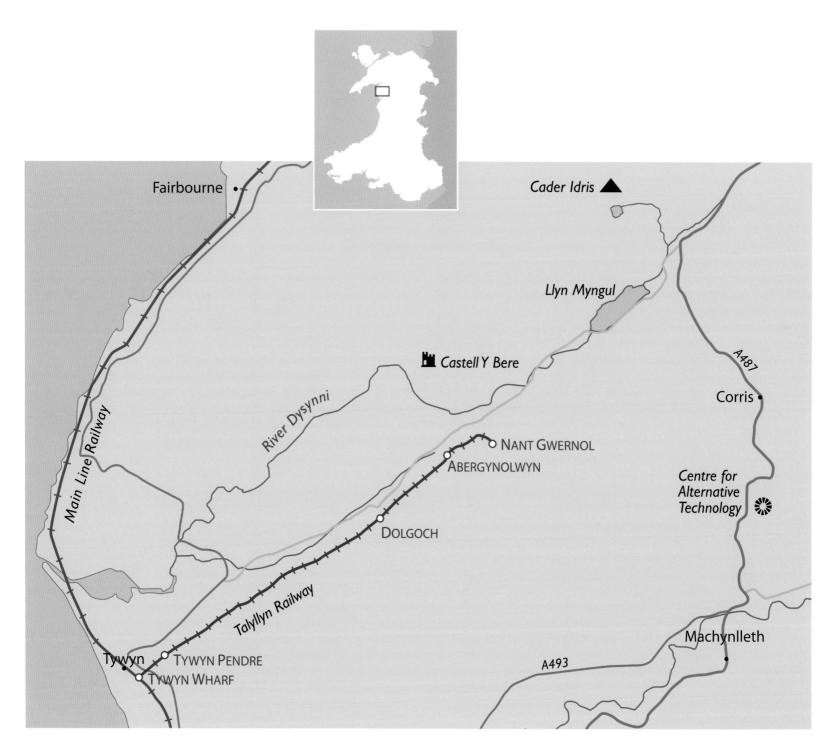

SOMEWHERE IN THE ATTIC AT HOME, beneath hand-me-down student kitchenware, old school books and end of term photographs there are boxes and boxes of model railways. They are all in their original packaging: green steam locomotives, brown and cream carriages, and miles and miles of track. A clear-out has been mooted a number of times, but my brothers and I are incapable of letting them go, even the damaged rails twisted after a childhood fight. The train sets were more important than life itself during days of rain in Pembrokeshire thirty years ago. The possibility that the next crop of Owens might want them (thus defying the experience of generations that children never want to play with their parents' toys) is trotted out as an excuse to postpone the day of reckoning.

Our model railways filled an entire room, the displays on uneven chipboard, complete with tunnels made from papier mâché stretched out over chicken wire. My Flying Scotsman, Huw's shunters and Richard's farmyard animals kept us quiet (most of the time) for the best part of ten years. And then one day, our all-consuming passion was abandoned; just like British Rail after Dr Beeching's cuts, the Owen railway came to the end of the line too. We discovered cars, and later girls, and our attic playroom fell silent. Childhood's like that, transient and fickle with its affections.

At the Talyllyn Railway they've never stopped playing with trains. I find something intriguing about the manic conviction of an adult railway enthusiast – I've watched them elsewhere from the safety of a train carriage – as they stand in the rain at the end of the platform in swivel-eyed excitement at the arrival of another delayed diesel. If for no other reason than to

Talyllyn Railway – for enthusiasts of all ages

Full steam

Rev. Awdry's study

forestall reprisals by the militant wing of the train spotters' union, I must point out that I am not unsentimental when it comes to old machinery. Over the years I've owned my fair share of unreliable elderly cars. But I've never really understood the passion of the train spotter.

Talyllyn is an intriguing riddle that defines the character of a nation. Why would you resuscitate a railway just as widespread car usage and the diesel train were coming into vogue in the 1950s? Why expend fortunes and lifetimes on a short journey to nowhere? (The whole trip is only seven miles.) But of course you will say that these are harsh and hard-headed questions that overlook our love of nostalgia, romance and delight in the absurd. We are comfortable with the past; in Britain we have hobbies in the way that other countries have religion and politics, and we are charmed by the eccentric. To dismiss the Talyllyn's followers as mere train-spotters would be foolish (if for no other reason than they know how to start a good fire).

All of which brings me to Tywyn, the home of Thomas the Tank Engine and friends. Few children could have grown up in the second half of the twentieth century and not have read about Thomas. Stories about the little steam engine began in 1943 when lifelong railway enthusiast the Reverend Wilbert Awdry created the tales for his three-year-old son Christopher who was recovering from measles. Christopher, like all children, demanded to be told the same stories again and again, and corrected his father when he allowed inconsistencies to creep in. So the Rev. Awdry began to write down the stories. But it was Mrs Awdry who believed the Thomas tales had mileage beyond the family home, and she nagged Wilbert to do something about it. In 1945 *The Three Railway Engines* appeared in print.

Reverend Wilbert was a stickler for continuity and was concerned that his new young readers, like Christopher, would write to him complaining if the stories were not consistent and realistic. To help him picture his new world, he created a fictional island called Sodor – between the Isle of Man and Cumbria – which would become the home of his fantasy railway.

They've recreated Wilbert's study at Talyllyn, with a map of the island hanging from the wall above the writer's desk – his empty pipe, spectacles and typewriter all left as though the vicar had just popped out to tea.

It's a tribute to Awdry, Thomas and the Talyllyn Railway – the inspiration for so many of the stories – that generations of children growing up in the age of diesel have become steam-engine enthusiasts. Later this morning, the station at Tywyn Wharf will be crowded with children coming to see their heroes. I'd be intrigued to witness their reaction when they see the tank engines face to face. It'll be a bit like meeting a long lost alcoholic uncle after many years, only to discover he's much fatter and foul smelling than you remember. But for now I have another more pressing appointment just down the track in the engine sheds at Pendre.

Pendre Works is the inner sanctum for the railway enthusiast, the vestry where the sacred vessels are kept. Its long, low, slate engine-shed is home to three cold locomotives, and in the darkness within, ministers a small army of busy volunteers. I'd expected the entire enterprise to be all about boys with toys, but there are converts of both sexes here, and in roughly equal numbers. By day Gareth Jones and Geoff Shuttleworth are consultants, holding down respectable jobs in town planning and environment services but this weekend, like most weekends, Saturday morning finds them exchanging office work for the grunge of steam. They are driver and fireman respectively of the tank engine No 2 *DOLGOCH*. Like many of the volunteers, they have both been coming to Talyllyn since they were little boys. There is no zeal like that of the young convert.

The dim whitewashed insides of the engine-shed have long given up any pretence to cleanliness; three tank engines stand behind each other over the

Dolgoch *crossing the viaduct*

PARALLEL LINES

When visitors to the Talyllyn Railway admire steam locomotives *Dolgoch* and *Duncan,* they may not realise that they are at the crossing point between fact and fiction. *Dolgoch* is part of the 'real' Talyllyn Railway, whilst *Duncan* (originally *Douglas*) belongs to its *doppelgänger*, the Skarloey Railway on the fictional island of Sodor. After falling in love with the line on a family holiday and working as a volunteer guard at Talyllyn, the Rev. W. Awdry based the history of the Skarloey Railway closely upon actual events at Talyllyn, and many of the real engines have fictional counterparts with Sudrian names. (*Dolgoch* reappears as *Rheneas* in the stories.)

The island of Sodor, which gives consistency to Awdry's fiction, not only has its own geography, but also its own history and language – a cross between Manx and Norse. The individual lines which make up the Skarloey Railway also have their own background stories with a history of amalgamations and line closures, with characters such as the Thin Controller and the Fat Controller boasting detailed biographies and employment histories.

Younger enthusiasts, less interested perhaps in the intricacies of the fictional universe, will be pleased to know that they can meet versions of the Fat Controller on location up and down Wales, as 'he' frequently makes guest appearances for special railway occasions. Nowadays more often referred to as Sir Topham Hat to ensure political correctness, the Fat Controller has even been mentioned in Hansard, with MPs using his name to lampoon real-life railway bigwigs. A case of life imitating art imitating life.

Duncan of the Skarloey Railway

Dolgoch of the Talyllyn Railway

inspection pit and wait for their daily engineering check, and later their fire and water. The stench of ancient grease and burnt iron grabs your nostrils. Lining the benches and hanging from the walls is an assortment of impossibly large tools that would be unfamiliar to a car mechanic.

Gareth finds me some blue overalls which look ridiculously clean beside everyone else's and Geoff hands me a pair of brand-new heavy-duty gloves. The dozen or so engineers, firemen, drivers and helpers have been here since before dawn. For the faithful, the calling is strong.

Gareth and Geoff have obviously decided that it's important for me to have the authentic experience. The first job I'm assigned is cleaning *Dolgoch*, which now that I'm standing closer to the engine, I can see is the size of a terraced house. Geoff hands me a rag and a tin of *Brasso*, and then proceeds to offer a master class in how to polish the brightwork without rubbing the grit into the shiny metal. I'm hoping that the director will realise that after we've got a few shots of this it won't be necessary to be detained for too long on the scrubbing, but to no avail. After what seems like an age, Gareth emerges with a cup of tea and, just like in the Thomas books, everything in the engine-shed comes to a halt for a brew. The preparation and care of the engines before they meet their public is meticulous, though my cuppa has a curious aftertaste of oil, but I don't like to say anything, in case it's the usual form here.

Polishing done and tea taken, it's time for duties on the footplate, the object of this morning's worship. Like a wise priest, Gareth gives me my first guided tour around the cab. It is cramped for two men, but as

In training

yet the iron is still cold to the touch. The huge brass pressure gauge dominates the instruments like a town clock with only one hand. Lower down is the air-pressure gauge; in the centre, the regulator which controls the speed – I'll never remember all this – the little injector wheel that brings water into the boiler; gauge glasses which indicate how much water is in the tanks; the steam brake, the air brake; an enormous gear lever offering two forward speeds and two reverse; and, suspended from the roof, a dangling chain to sound the whistle (this is the only one of the controls that I understand). With each fond gesture of explanation Gareth wipes each instrument in turn with his rag, although he may just as well have talked in Urdu; this is an unfamiliar and foreign place. I'm hoping he won't expect me to recall any of it. Gareth disappears with his oil can to lubricate No. 2, as Geoff arrives at the footplate to begin my fire-making lesson.

With a handful of diesel-soaked rags, a few lumps of coal and small pieces of wood for kindling, we huddle over to make a fire on the face of the shovel, before dropping the flaming contents into the cold belly of *Dolgoch*. The rags catch light quickly and soon too the kindling wood, all of it gently dropped through the fire door. Geoff explains the key to a good fire is to make sure it's evenly spread. So my first shovelful from the coal bunker at the side of the cab is placed at the far back of the firebox, the next one to the sides, then in the middle, and the last loads are placed just inside the warming door. Then a few bone-dry lumps of broken fencing post go into the inferno. The coal is from Poland, and a bad load yesterday caused an engine to clinker up. Within a few minutes, the ironwork around

Feeding the hungry beast

the fire door becomes hot, and fuelling this hungry monster with coal and wood is like hand-feeding a sharp-toothed bulldog. I can feel the hair on my wrists singeing. Note to self to wear gloves at all times.

As the temperature on the footplate rises, the needle on the pressure gauge flickers off its cold pin, and some two hours after I arrive, No. 2 is finally fired up and ready to go. (You can see why someone invented a diesel train with a turn start.) Gareth is handed a crisp white-typed note with his instructions for the day. But our first journey is only a few yards into the bright sunshine to the water tower and coal stocks.

Dolgoch hisses to a halt below the hose and Geoff fills the water tank in just a few minutes. But our next task takes considerably longer on account of my lack of experience in the shovelling department (unless you count working in a newsroom). Filling the seemingly bottomless bunker of a tank engine takes an age. By the end of refuelling, my hands are shaking with the unfamiliar strain of loading tons and tons of heavy steam coal. We haven't gone anywhere yet and yours truly's already knackered. I'm ready to admit that honest toil like this does not form part of my day-to-day existence as a journalist.

Around the sheds, polishing and watching, is a gathering of teenagers in overalls – too young yet to work on board, but nonetheless the next generation of converts ready to continue the mission.

Behind us on the line, the readied *Sir Haydn* is resplendent in red. Before moving off for duties typed on yet another crisp white sheet of paper, he slowly comes to the boil. He spits past us like an angry kettle.

Plenty of brass to polish

JONES Y GUARD

Dyn siriol a dawn siarad – yw efe
Yn y Van yn wastad;
Enwog wr, llawn o gariad
Ar y lein yn gweini'r wlad.

A cheerful word for every man
Has Jones, the guardian of the Van,
His love of country, rain or shine,
Expressed in service on the line.

Hedd Wyn (1887-1917)

Edward Thomas, *like* Sir Haydn, *formerly of the Corris Railway*

Underneath the arches

My coaling and water done, it's time to hop up to the hissing cab which is now almost unbearably hot. Gareth and Geoff look back through the glass portholes in the rear wall to watch for a signal from the blockman. He will wave for us to reverse through the sidings over the main line and cross to the shed with the carriages that are to make up our train.

'Beware of Locomotives' it says on a huge white iron sign stuck to the stone wall with rusted bolts. It would be difficult indeed to miss those shrieking hulks ambling over the points.

As one of the original locomotives of the Talyllyn, No. 2 *Dolgoch* will pull hundreds of years of Welsh railway history today: we're to couple with a carriage from the Corris Railway, the four original four-wheel Talyllyn carriages from the 1860s, a plush four-wheel First Class carriage from the 1890s from the Glyn Valley Tramway, and the original brake van with booking-office from the 1860s. Gareth gently noses *Dolgoch* into the first carriage's coupling; Geoff directs him, standing beside the rails and shouting pointlessly

above the din, then finally fastens up the enormous chains and hose that make us all one. I watch him and pretend I know what he's doing.

Back aboard the footplate, the three of us crowd into the little cab and turn to face the empty rails through the round windows behind us. Gareth coaxes No. 2 to pull the small toy-like carriages down the line from Pendre to Wharf station, where our passengers wait. Once there, we will, for the second but by no means the last time today, uncouple the carriages so the engine can cross into a parallel siding and then potter round to the front of the train.

A hiss, a whistle and we arrive at Wharf. The thick stench of smoke is evidently a surprise to some of the waiting crowd, busily taking pictures one minute and coughing up their lungs the next.

I have to admit that any opportunity to leave the baking furnace of the footplate is going to be welcome, and as we will stand at Wharf platform for a while, I'm going to nip out for a nose around the carriages and the station.

The crowds come to Tywyn chiefly for the beach and the Talyllyn Railway. But the town's also home to another treat: the church of St Cadfan boasts the earliest example of written Welsh, engraved on a stone dating back to AD 650.

But today the faithful are reading words and numbers of a different kind, mouthing quietly to themselves from a timetable on the edge of town. Tywyn Wharf is the main passenger terminus, but was originally the transfer point for slate carried from Bryn Eglwys Quarry in the hills above Abergynolwyn. The Talyllyn narrow gauge railway transferred its loads here onto the standard gauge Cambrian main line. (That scared you – I sounded like a railway bore for a moment.)

The passengers standing on the platform hesitate before getting onto the train as if they might be making a mistake and boarding the wrong one, even though this is the only service. There are no announcements and no electronic notice-boards, just a booming station master whose reassuring voice has them scurrying to twist the huge brass handles to open the under-sized doors. They've left behind on the platform tables a veritable canteen of white china cups and saucers, and plates of half-eaten cakes.

The first passengers clambered aboard the Talyllyn in December 1866, soon after William McConnel, a Manchester businessman, opened the doors. The slate quarry at Bryn Eglwys was prosperous especially in the 1880s, but was in decline by the 1900. Then unexpectedly, came a huge leap in profits as quarrymen in north Wales went on strike. The Penrhyn strike caused so much demand for slate that these years were the most prosperous for Bryn Eglwys and for the railway. So when McConnel sold to Sir Henry Haydn Jones in 1911, his profits were substantial.

When Sir Henry Haydn Jones died in 1950, the future of the Talyllyn looked bleak. A small band of volunteers was determined to save the line and the Talyllyn Railway Preservation Society was born. Among its earliest supporters were the poet John Betjeman and the Reverend Wilbert Awdry.

Clutching brown and cream tickets behind the windows, the passengers of 2006 look out of place in the formal Victorian hand-painted carriages, their garish shell suits and England football tops jarring and out of time. First Class (an extra two pounds supplementary fare) is padded in blue leather upholstery and has a deep

Bryn Eglwys Quarry; signal box

Dolgoch

red carpet. White-crested headrests protect the leather from the greasy heads of the unwashed, and, suspended just below the top of the carriage, the brass-capped luggage nets are too small to hold anything larger than a handbag. In the ceiling, a large white glass globe is a shining centrepiece that wouldn't last two minutes on today's railways. The Third Class carriage has wooden benches and looks uncomfortable even for an hour's ride, not that this seems to deter those who huddle inside, enjoying a masochist's away day.

Back on the footplate, a whistle and a flag from the guard and we're off. Gareth, through scorched gloves, caresses levers and taps. A vast hissing energy is slipped into gear. Behind us, passing slowly at first, another swarm of passengers rushes onto the empty platform ready for the next service and we move away in a controlled explosion of fire, water and steam. One of the world's shortest railway journeys has begun, and I'm watching it all from the splendour of the footplate.

Within seconds of departure, the train is plunged momentarily into darkness as we waddle slowly under the road bridge, which, because of our slow pace, gives the impression that it's more tunnel-like than it really is, all of which brings squeals of excitement to each successive carriage.

After the level crossing at Tywyn Pendre, the bulging hills around Tŷ Mawr look yellowed in the hottest summer for years. Close to the line, some streetwise sheep continue chewing without looking up at the smoke and steam passing by.

At Fach-goch, they're gathering in the hay and the fields look hastily shorn – a few tufts left behind here and there by a careless barber. In the next field a

All aboard

At the foot of Mynydd Pentre

chestnut horse nervously trots away from the streak of acrid plume before looking back to check that the danger has passed.

An ash tree, huge, stands alone in the acre below Cynfal farm; it looks just like the plastic ones I had on my train set, motionless and still without any wind to worry it. And behind us, edging back at walking pace, the vast light blue-grey of Cardigan Bay.

There is something wonderfully soothing about the sound of a railway and its rhythmic swaying. It's comforting – like being rocked to sleep in a cot – and drowns out any thought. It is a moment to watch the world without thinking too much about it.

I had hoped to continue my journey, hanging out the side of the cab, swallowing warm air and soot, to escape

the heat of the footplate but Geoff has other ideas. To a railwayman, the scenery is no more than a distraction and an obstacle. There is coal to be shovelled, steam to be built and an incline to climb. My paternal grandfather was an engine driver on the Great Western from London to Pembroke Dock. I've never given his life much thought; now I realise how physically fit he and his friends must have been to withstand eight hours on the footplate, much of that time shovelling coal into a bottomless ball of fire. Balancing on a moving train whilst throwing coal into a furnace is something I'm glad I don't have to do for a living, or for that matter, a hobby. Geoff says he's pleased with the pressure and to my great relief, after a few more shovelfuls, my coaling duties are finished, at least for a while. They might be mad this lot, but they're fit and mad.

Our wheezing clickety-clicking brings out a crowd of waving children who rush to the fence to greet the train like we used to do at my grandparents' cottage in Saundersfoot. The other side of the hedge is home to a camping park full of caravans painted green to help them blend into the grass.

We are climbing all the time now and the engine note is one of constant strain. James Spooner's track is two feet three inches wide with an average gradient of 1 in 160. It runs for 7¼ miles which roughly translates as uphill-all-the-way and downhill-all-the-way back.

At Rhydyronen station, a sweating rag in hand, Gareth pushes the regulator gently; a hiss and a slowing of clicks on the tracks means we're stopping to wait for the down train to pass.

In a few minutes, *The Quarryman* whooshes in the other direction within inches of *Dolgoch*; it's laden with tourists but its engine sounds unburdened as it heads down valley. A signalman in blue uniform stands poised, hand outstretched, ready to exchange a token with us. This is my job – and I pretend to understand what I'm doing. I hang out of the moving train to reach out for a huge key that allows us passage up the line. Fortunately, we're going slowly enough for another go at catching it, should it all go wrong. But I grab it first time and we pick up speed.

More coal shovelling, and Gareth and Geoff seem pleased that I have done my fair share of the donkey work without too much shirking. They exude a calm and inner peace despite the ferocious heat. It's difficult to imagine meeting people who appear more content with their lot: they wear a seemingly permanent grin.

My reward, they say, for good behaviour, will be to drive the engine for the next stretch of line. I suddenly feel both delighted and worried; having taking the mickey out of them for their private passion, I find myself privately thrilled at the prospect of driving a steam engine myself, and at the same time concerned that I can't remember anything of Gareth's teaching in the engine-shed. But this is too good an opportunity to refuse and we change places. For someone brought up to drive cars, this really couldn't be more different. Each instrument seems outsize, its action heavy over the flames. It feels like handling a branding iron; the entire cab has soaked the heat of the fire and is almost too hot to touch.

What an experience! Gareth motions to pull 'her' back into second gear. The lever looks like something that the BBC would use to control a small country's transmitters. But 'she' responds well, and with a caress of the regulator, we edge towards our maximum speed

Token for passage up the line

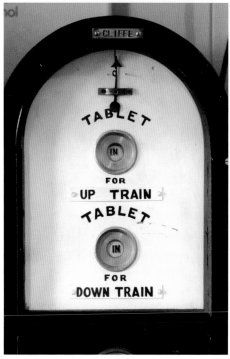

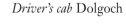

Driver's cab Dolgoch

of twelve miles per hour. I'm grinning uncontrollably. A white and black sign at the side of the track says 'Whistle' and like an indulgent elder brother, Gareth nods for me to grab the chain. The din from the engine is by now too loud to hear any screams of fear from my passengers. But I can't look back; I am lost in this moment. The Talyllyn mob are worse than an extremist sect: I've been brainwashed and converted – they've made a train-spotter out of me when I wasn't looking and it is both wonderful and dangerously addictive.

My steam-engine driving experience is too short lived. Brynglas station is coming into sight and Gareth takes over to prevent the Talyllyn's first disaster. It was brief but marvellous. Stepping out onto the platform, I feel I've become one of the chosen, rather than one of the passengers. Over the picket fence, the landscape throughout the Fathew valley looks like a bleached water-colour painting; the only bright green this August is the engine's paint, now flecked with black smuts. The trees and their fields crave rain, absent now for weeks. On the river banks below, a hundred gulls follow a tractor ploughing the dry dust, hoping for unearthed fat worms in the shocked soil.

Brynglas station is full of bewildered passengers who got on a train to nowhere in particular and now find they have no idea of where they are. Not that the destination really matters on the Talyllyn; this is a journey for its own sake, for smells and sights rather than arrival. Parents push their children to stand near *Dolgoch*'s buffers, but their initial thrill is crushed by smoke and heat and the disappointment of a tank engine who doesn't talk. That will be one unsmiling photograph for the family album. *Our holiday in Wales.*

MARY JONES – THREE FOR THE PRICE OF ONE

The name Mary Jones should be instantly forgettable in a country which claims a record number of Joneses. But in the minds of Welsh people, the name Mary Jones signifies one very special woman. Born to poor parents in the village of Llanfihangel-y-Pennant in the middle of the eighteenth century, Mary Jones's determination to acquire a Bible is the stuff of legend.

Mary's mother was a woman of great piety. Widowed young, she used to take her small daughter with her to religious meetings, sometimes letting her hold the lantern to light the lonely pathway. As a ten-year-old Mary was lucky enough to attend the circulating school established by Thomas Charles at Abergynolwyn. A circulating school would stay in an area for a couple of months before moving on. The aim was to teach children to read and instruct them in the principles of the Christian faith.

Mary was a good student but her family was too poor to have a Bible at home. She used to visit Penybryniau Mawr, a farm some miles away, where the farmer's wife let her read the family Bible. Mary was very anxious to have her own copy and saved up every spare penny. One day, as she made her way to Penybryniau, she bumped into Thomas Charles himself. When he discovered why she was making the journey, he told her that he would be able to supply her with a Bible at his home in Bala where he was expecting a new stock of Welsh Bibles from London.

After saving up enough money, Mary made the long journey – twenty-five miles – to Bala on foot, but she was in for a disappointment. The promised Bibles hadn't arrived and wouldn't do so for a further two days. Fortunately, Mary was able to find lodgings and, when the precious delivery arrived, Thomas Charles gave her three Bibles for the price of one.

Dyssynni valley towards Llanfihangel-y-Pennant

Monument at Mary Jones's home

Jeremy Moore

Dyfed Elis-Gruffydd

Jeremy Moore

Above: Dôl-goch viaduct; below: Castell y Bere

All aboard again. An elderly rosy-cheeked station master in a wonderful uniform has been waiting all his life to blow the whistle; he completes his task with aplomb and looks around for approval.

The train slips back for a moment, before stammering forward like a father carrying a heavy child. From here to Dolgoch Falls station, the track grips precariously to the side of the hill. The flashes of sunlight, which have washed the cab for the last hour, disappear as the forest of trees thickens and envelops the train. I catch sight of my reflection in the glass porthole and I look filthier than I can ever remember – smuts from the smoke cover my face and my blue shirt is blackened.

Over Dôl-goch viaduct, the cascading water of the falls below goes unnoticed by our passengers. Another whistle, then Gareth brings No. 2 to a scraping halt on the rails at Dolgoch Falls station. A handful of walkers drag their rucksacks out of the narrow carriage doors. They squint at their maps before striking out through the canopy of leaves.

Three generations of the same family – grandfather, son and grandchildren – all rush to the side of the engine for photographs before we pull off again. This is in the blood; this enthusiasm is like being born to crack addicts; if your parents are into steam – there's no chance of escaping the genes.

Over the hill behind Foel Cae'rberllan is the ruined fortress of Castell y Bere, built by Llywelyn the Great to secure the route through the mountains and the ancient Kingdom of Gwynedd. Its isolated romantic beauty still draws passengers to walk around its stones. And beside it is the tiny hamlet of Llanfihangel-y-Pennant the birthplace of Mary Jones who two hundred years ago walked barefoot to Bala to find a Bible printed in Welsh.

A few miles further on, deep in the forest between Mynydd Rhiwerfa and Foel Fach, a waistcoated signalman looks out from his high clapperboard perch; this is Abergynolwyn station. He's a retired parish priest who has taken up another career that offers a journey, a timetable, regulations and a hot fire at the end of it all. He jokes that both the railway and the church think they are best placed to get you to your destination. His pulpit now contains a dozen waist-high silver levers and an ancient telephone that doesn't ring.

Some five miles north-east of Abergynolwyn station, is the mountaineer's Mecca: mighty Cadair Idris, where King Arthur lives. At Tal-y-llyn, on the floor of Dysynni valleys south of the summit, lies the lake prized by trout and salmon fishermen: Llyn Myngul. But only a few will be exploring either of these wonders of Wales. Although most passengers get off at each station, they then get back on again after having a look around and stretching their legs. It is the railway alone that most have come to explore.

Nant Gwernol station, our journey's end, is carved into the cliff and offers a half-hour stop to allow the engine to uncouple and run around to the back of the carriages. In the railway's heyday, passengers never came here; this stop was only to load the quarry's slate onto the wagons.

Some older children snap photos with their mobile phones or stand impassively, indulging their fathers' whims. The quarry, a short walk from here, dominated the local slate industry of the nineteenth century.

Dôl-goch Falls

Llyn Myngul, Tal-y-llyn

When John Pughe first began quarrying at Bryn Eglwys, the slates were carried by pack horses to Aberdyfi for shipment. Some twenty years later the Aberdovey Slate Company expanded the place and needed a railway to carry the material to Tywyn. In the quarry's heyday in 1880s three hundred men were employed the hills, although for much of its history both quarry and railway were unprofitable. Now the quarry is silent and left to the ghosts.

Two dogs on leads begin to fight on the platform; their owners strangle them apart.

Geoff goes for the tea and Gareth grabs some air on the platform to hide from the really serious railway enthusiasts clucking at the footplate, cameras and notebooks in hand.

'Just imagine if we didn't have our railway,' he says. 'We'd be out in the community with time on our hands.' He laughs and jumps back in the cab.

Slowly passengers wander back to the trains with the exception of two heavy-booted walkers loaded with rucksacks. They sit on a bench for a moment to watch us steam off.

Once these rails would have carried wagons of slate for roofing, and gravestones too, larger cuts to make billiard tables or smaller pieces to fashion school writing tablets. From Tywyn much of the slate was transported on the main-line Cambrian railway as far as Aberdyfi, where it would be loaded on to coastal sailing ships and taken to ports around the coast of Britain and Ireland.

For the return journey, I'm going to climb aboard the carriages to enjoy the trip as a passenger. In the seats behind me, a picnic begins; a bag of apples, packets of crisps and chocolate bars quieten a rowdy brood. Then, with a flag and whistle (and an answering toot from the cab), the tall guard, resplendent in black cap and long coat, signals the long roll back out of the station.

Our carriages are full of excited anticipation, bubbling with stories of a splendid adventure to tell back at home. We don't like our adventures to be too unpredictable in Wales, and the Talyllyn delivers a great British railway journey, a steam engine and a refreshing cup of tea. On these hard wooden benches, bouncing along this Victorian railway, I wonder what it is about us that makes us more comfortable with the past. Of all the tourist attractions you'll find in Wales I'll bet the majority are not science parks celebrating the future, but time capsules of a lost age like this one.

Back in my carriage a difficult conversation begins between two small children and their parents about whether Thomas and his friends are real as they didn't reply when spoken to at the platform. No doubt, a difficult drive home lies ahead when God and Father Christmas are also put to closer examination. But doubt and heresy are for the young. For my part, the Talyllyn has woven its spell and I too have become a believer.

Dyfed Elis-Gruffydd

Cader Idris

SPLENDOURS OF CADER IDRIS

As I climbed Cader Idris with a friend last Sunday I thought of Thomas Pennant, who in 1773 was one of the first to describe an ascent of this mountain. He struck a wet day and got no view. But he was able to look down into those glacial cirques that have gouged out precipices on either side of the narrow summit ridge. He saw them as 'a sort of theatre with a lake at the bottom'. He was also impressed by the chaos of naked rocks that lay in all directions; and quite astutely for those early days he suggested that these rocks might have come out of a volcano . . . Cader gets deservedly more popular year by year. My companion on Sunday was a Canadian lady with experience of far higher mountains than those of Britain. Yet she found Cader Idris full of appeal because its rugged treelessness gives it true mountain qualities. In North America there are many ranges that are disappointing to climb because they are forested to the summit and give you no view at all. But from Cader on a clear day you see across all Snowdonia and central Wales to similar bare heights, all of which are marvellous viewpoints. You would need a long lifetime to visit every one of them.

William Condry (1918-1998) *A Welsh Country Diary*

Cader Idris and Llyn Myngul, Tal-y-llyn

Jeremy Moore

SAILING
TO THE
SEVERN

STORM AND SUNSHINE

We have the sea to ourselves and I know why – away from the safety of the harbour the ocean is in cruel mood and intent on lashing all who sail on her. Richard the film cameraman keeps bracing himself with his legs against the bulkhead while trying to hold his camera steady. We are all clipped onto the safety lines running the length of the vessel, but they won't save us from being thrown around on deck; they merely prevent us from being washed too far away.

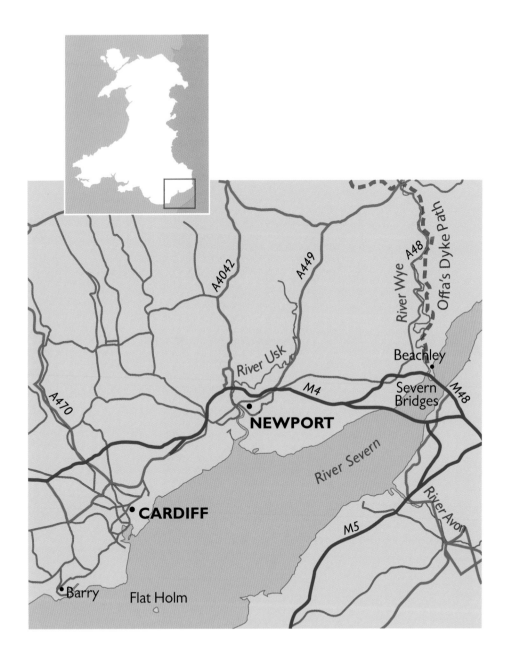

IT'S EARLY ON SATURDAY AND BARRY IS still asleep on a cold day in June that is as dark and frowning as winter. The stationary fairground rides of the amusement park on Barry Island look bleak and slightly sinister. The crowds and their screams won't arrive for many hours. We came here on school-trips and even then found the attractions to be over the hill and tired. The place is a bit like an end-of-the-pier entertainer whose act has run for too many seasons. But the scruffiness is slowly being brushed away; the developer's plans don't carry the baggage of memories – they stress only the potential of real estate with ocean views. The waterside apartments are shooting up here as everywhere else along this coast, though these flats lack the grace and splendour of some of their Victorian neighbours.

I've sailed around the Welsh coast a few times, but I have never explored the stretch of water east of here to the River Severn. On each of my previous voyages I've turned right out of Cardiff and headed west. My plan had been to put this glaring omission right and sail from Barry to Flat Holm island then onto Newport and up the Bristol Channel to the River Severn. But a furtive look around the gathering television crew confirms my suspicions. The forecast is terrible – force 7 winds are expected, the light is low like those watery dim days in January, and our brief to film a landscape documentary to showcase the coast is looking precarious. We will have to work hard today to capture this glowering corner of Wales in its best light. It looks miserable and grim.

A few miles out to sea is David Heal, the owner of *Swansong*, who set off before first light from Swansea, along with an accompanying yacht. He and his crew will have endured hours of slamming into angry waves trying to make progress at walking pace to meet us by nine o'clock. David's yacht, a beautiful craft of thirty-five feet, is better suited to what we have planned than a bigger boat. It has a shallow draught and is capable of getting up rivers and onto shores. But on a day like this it won't be much fun facing the growing anger of the open ocean in a light craft.

David is heading here to Barry to collect us: three of us for his boat and another film crew for the other yacht in order to get the wide angles of our boat.

Do we call the whole thing off and send everyone home, or plough on? Dozens of people have given up their weekends to help us film, including two yacht crews who have been through one of the most gruelling trips of the summer. We have all shot enough sailing documentaries to know how dangerous filming can be in bad weather. You can hold onto the boat if it gets rough on a normal voyage but with a film crew on board in addition to the yacht crew, the whole operation becomes more crowded and risky. Delay it, though, and we know we could come back here next week to retry and, in this bizarrely changing climate, have the same dilemma.

Everyone quickly comes to the same conclusion: we will begin the voyage and if the weather turns any worse, return to Barry. There are six of us who have worked on this series for months and been together for years on others. There comes a time when, like squabbling married couples, you all know each other so well that you know what the other is thinking. Right now I know that Richard and Tony the cameramen and

Above: Flat Holm; below: Swansong *on a choppy sea*

Leaving Barry

Martin the photographer will climb aboard shortly because they don't want to let people down. A grim determination fixes over their faces. This is going to be soaking, dangerous and possibly even a thrilling day. Another adventure beckons, like those roller-coaster rides when you were little; you don't really want to do it because it's scary, but you clamber on, defying your reason, because you like to be scared.

In the stubborn mist of early morning, two masts poke the leaden horizon. We won't have to ask David and the two crews if they have had a good trip. From the harbour wall we can see them huddled and silent, like watch officers on the bridge. Their wet weather gear is soaked and their progress so painfully slow that their final mile seems to take an age, as tide and waves throw them in any direction other than their chosen course.

With both yachts finally tied to a mooring, David steps into an impossibly small inflatable dingy to make the short hop to the stone jetty. The jetty's crowded with waiting film crew, piles of tapes, cameras, equipment boxes and provisions. It takes three shuttles before we're all sorted.

Climbing back on board the yacht at last, David yells an offer to '. . . show you where everything is', but it's lost in a howl of wind.

Swansong is virtually brand-new and David begins his guided tour with enthusiasm that he is beginning to recover from his earlier trial at sea. The saloon is beautifully fitted out in wood and expensive fittings, but on a day like today its quarters will be avoided, so as to lessen the chances of motion sickness.

After the safety drills, emergency flares and life-jacket demonstration, we cast off from Barry's mooring and turn out of the comforting arms of the harbour. The brawling sea is now lit by glorious sunshine but it fails to heat the cold air.

Flat Holm is only a few miles offshore, its brooding hulk like a surfacing whale. The daily service boat makes the journey in under an hour, but we will be making our way against tides, currents and winds that have no wish for visitors today.

The lighthouse at Barry shrinks behind us as we alternately race on a squall and then almost stop at the whim of the tide. Beside us, Sully Bay is empty and a lone walker clings to Hopkins Mount clad in purple waterproofs visible for miles against the grey.

There is something wonderfully exhilarating about setting sail on a yacht, even in these conditions. It's the ancient union of wind and ropes. For all this yacht's brimming technology of GPS satellite positioning and automatic pilot, it's not very different from what sailing a boat has always been – man trying to harness nature's power to the best of his abilities. But this morning we know who has the upper hand.

'I'm getting what I can,' reports Richard. This is cameraman-speak in the company of others to say, 'this caper is hopeless and we're wasting our time'.

This is an extraordinary day – at the same time that waves are breaking over the hull soaking us to the skin, we are also passing the sun-cream around to save burning our faces in the early glare. The rather quiet mood of departure has now been broken by a few laughs after each of us in turn takes another wave in the face. It's rather like one of those slapstick comedies where buckets of water are continuously thrown over the characters.

A lurching horizon

David asks me to take over at the wheel for a while. We think it'll take nearly two hours to do our filming and get to Flat Holm and we'll all take the helm at some stage. Standing behind this massive silver steering-wheel, holding onto the cold metal circle, you wonder if it's your hands that are really holding the yacht's course or if the sails have entered into a pact with the wind and reduced you to a fearful spectator. Now I can feel the brutal and unkind strength of the sea and it's shaking my fingers as I try to tame its mad rage. Another wave breaks over our heads and soon small streams of freezing salt water find their way through the waterproofs and down my back.

Only sailors and drunks will understand that disorientation that comes when the horizon is knocked from you. I didn't see it coming, but like a prowling tiger, an immense wave attacks, yanking our yacht out of the sea. I don't know whether it was the wave or tripping into the vacuum of air left in its wake, but it knocked all of us from our feet and unseated Richard and Martin who were trying to look down their lenses. Is this the turning point where we give up and return

home? No programme that we make is worth serious injury and the assignment will be pointless if their cameras are no longer functioning. Martin speaks first: 'I'm fine,' and then Richard: 'The camera is fine,' and then they laugh, bonded in adversity. We are grimly determined to carry on now that the endurance test has begun in earnest.

There is a fine line between exhilaration and danger and we have just passed it. For a moment I know what that adrenaline buzz must be like for Formula One drivers, jockeys and adventure sport junkies. It's about achievement for the sake of achievement's sake, a mountain to climb simply because it's there, and a yacht adventure because it'll test us all.

After an hour, the swell of the waves becomes less fierce – the sea cuts us some slack for passing its initiation test. We prepare to change direction and 'go about' before landing on Flat Holm. The last time I was here it was dawn on *Mascotte* – the century-old Bristol Channel cutter. Any change to her direction or sails meant all hands on deck and heavy manual labour

to pull ropes and pulleys. On *Swansong* a hundred years of technological innovation means the same operation is light and easy; this yacht could be sailed solo. But after our crash into the big wave I wish only for a moment that we were all on *Mascotte*'s massive hulk, rather than on this lighter speed machine.

On Flat Holm's shelf, the dingy shuttles us to the island, and the wind that made the journey here so harsh begins to drop with each step up the cliff. It's turning into the most beautiful morning. From here the skyline of Cardiff is striking, the Millennium Stadium like a child's Meccano construction, and just off the mainland a dozen red-sailed dinghies dip their toes in the water.

Julie Furber is the young warden of Flat Holm. Today her duties will include bidding goodbye to a samba band from London booked in for a few days to a rehearsal venue that will guarantee no complaints. She will later guide a variety of kagool-wearing bird-spotters to peek at full nests of eggs expected to hatch any day; and she has already marshalled the Barry Amateur Radio Society members to their allotted place in the sun.

'How long have you got?' she asks, knowing the answer will mean a change of the schedule we had planned on the phone. 'That's what island living is all about,' she smiles, whisking us off on the edited highlights tour.

Flat Holm was awarded Site of Special Scientific Interest status in 1972 in recognition of the island's gull population, the rare maritime grass species and the geological formation of the island and its intertidal zone.

Walking towards the path back to the jetty, a samba drummer laden down with his instruments and rucksack pauses to thank Julie for her hospitality. Then like a teacher on a school-trip for reprobates, she leads us briskly onto the lighthouse.

'If we stood here ten thousand years ago,' she continues, 'Flat Holm was a hill in the midst of a wooded valley and some species still survive from that time.'

The squat lighthouse is silent and its light won't be needed today. From the sixth century the island was used as a place of religious retreat and farming, and then in Victorian times it was heavily fortified. Flat Holm is littered with scruffy ruins. As is the way on islands, broken buildings rarely get removed but are left to deteriorate in wind and weather.

It's difficult to imagine that such a small stretch of land could cram so much of Britain's life story onto such a compact space. In the 1880s, the farm buildings were used as a cholera hospital, and then further fortifications came again in the Second World War when Flat Holm was one of the last chances to pick out enemy planes before they attacked the docks. But

Above: Oystercatchers; below: Perching on the ruins

FLAT HOLM LIGHTHOUSE

Flat Holm lies in a very busy sea area where the Severn Estuary meets the Bristol Channel. Small wonder then that there were calls for a lighthouse many years before the first light was established there in 1737. In fact, it took a tragedy – the loss of sixty souls in 1736 – and some hard bargaining by the island's lessee, William Crispe, and the Bristol-based Society of Merchant Venturers, before a lighthouse in the modern sense could be erected at all. (It is likely that there were crude attempts to show a light from early times, probably in the form of a simple brazier.) After 1737, all shipping using the Bristol Channel – with the exception of market and fishing boats – had to pay a toll, with a graduated scale of charges for vessels sailing overseas or to Ireland, and those sailing from St David's Head or Land's End.

Flat Holm's lighthouse had a rocky career in its early days, buffeted equally by financial and by meteorological storms. On 23 December 1790 the light was struck by lightning, sustaining considerable damage, the man in charge of the fire nearly falling through the stairway.

The corporation of Trinity House – the body responsible even today for aids to navigation, from lighthouses to radar beacons – agreed to take charge of Flat Holm's lighthouse, making improvements to its design and maintenance from 1819 onwards. Thereafter, newer and ever more sophisticated equipment was installed and the light was automated in 1988. In later years two teams of three keepers worked in relays, maintaining the three-man Trinity House practice established after the Smalls tragedy. (The Smalls, a remote lighthouse off the Pembrokeshire coast, had been inhabited by two quarrelsome keepers, one of whom died. His partner was driven mad when, terrified that he would be blamed for his colleague's death, he tied the body to the outside of the lighthouse in a makeshift coffin. Marooned by fierce storms, he was then doomed for weeks to watch the dead keeper's arm flapping in the gale.)

In recent times the residents of Cardiff and the Vale have been pleased to hear the familiar tones of the foghorn – set up originally in a separate building in 1908 but silent for some years – now restored to full power and ready to sound for special occasions.

for all the history on Flat Holm, what is most important today is the birds.

Julie's words are delivered to an increasingly spaced-out line of followers straggling a long way behind her, desperately trying to keep pace while carrying the filming gear.

'Does she know what we've been through to get here?' Martin asks, breathing heavily.

Then to great relief, at last she stops at a closed gate. The gate marks the boundary between the relatively short grass of half of the island and the wild reserve given over to nature on the other. Bizarrely the birds seem to know which half is theirs. It's as though someone has drawn a line down Flat Holm. On one side of the fence the island is home to the lighthouse and old farmhouse and then beyond the fence the dense undergrowth hides one of Britain's most significant concentrations of birdlife. This is their domain.

The nests are full of eggs and the young are days away from hatching. Their parents don't want anyone near them.

The alarmed gulls, fearful of predators, behave like some politicians under threat; they are frighteningly aggressive, terribly noisy and, as a last resort, fly as close to you as possible – and then shit on you. If you saw grown men cowering on Flat Holm one summer's day, it was us ducking from the threat of thousands of birds who were none too impressed with their unwelcome visitors.

Nesting gulls are not the only occasional visitors to Flat Holm today. Well away from the deafening shriek of the birds, in the overgrown back garden of the old farmhouse, you'll find a woolly-bearded amateur radio

enthusiast. Glyn Jones is sitting alongside his mate Ken Eaton and for one weekend every year they recreate a little bit of broadcasting history here.

Sitting at a makeshift table holding scanners, microphones, headphones and a small satellite dish, they call out to anyone who might be listening. This is the broadcasting equivalent of a blind date. They have no idea who is listening or where they are, unless they choose to identify themselves, which some do. After a few minutes of unrequited appeals, we are joined by a Russian near Moscow who speaks no English, and then a Scot in Edinburgh who does.

Glyn and Ken invite me to have a go. I've never understood the thrill of the amateur radio world and my suggestion to use a mobile phone instead leaves them a little crestfallen. But after a few minutes I can begin to see why they spend all their time and money on this endeavour. Their efforts to stretch a few more technological boundaries are in the same spirit that fired Marconi many years ago.

Lesser black backed gull amid thrift; Glyn Jones; Escorting musicians to the jetty

. . . I got down in good time to my Cardiff Steamer; a brisk breezy morning promising well: and again after endless ringing of bells and loading of hampers, and bullying and jumbling, in which I took part only as a distant onlooker, we got off down the muddy Avon once more. I passed a most silent day, remembrances of all kinds and these only my occupation. On the Somersetshire shore we passed a bathing-establishment: hapless Mothers of families sitting on the folding-stools by the beach of muddy tide-streams, Ach Gott! It is a solitary sea the Severn one; we

Severn Estuary at Goldcliff

Aled Hughes

passed near only one ship, and in that there lay a cabin boy sound asleep amid ropes, and a black-visaged sailor had raised his shock-head only half awake, thro' the hatches, to see what we were: they lay there waiting for a wind. I smoked 2 cigars and a half; I hummed all manner of tunes, sang even portions of Psalms in a humming tone for my own behoof, reclining on my elbow; and so the day wore on, and at three o'clock we got into Cardiff dock.

Thomas Carlyle (1795-1881)

On May 13th 1897, Marconi used Flat Holm in his first radio transmission across water to Lavernock Point three miles away. Once signals had been successfully received – which no doubt took a bit of fiddling with the aerial – a telegraphic message was sent to Queen Victoria at her home on the Isle of Wight. Those who watched this precocious advance in communication – which involved signals coming out of the air without wires – must have been dumbstruck.

Marconi is reported to have said, 'The calm of my life from this moment has ended.' He also predicted that one day man would communicate with the stars.

'Last year we communicated with the International Space Station from Flat Holm,' says Ken. So the stars are not such a fantasy after all.

The advice from our own yacht radio this morning, of course, was not to hang around, so it's back on the dinghy. I know that our brief visit short-changed Flat Holm; it's a fascinating island full of many more stories. But Newport and the Severn are calling.

All passengers back safely on board, tender fastened, anchor up and we set a new course. Flat Holm glides slowly past at first until the wind finds our sails and throws us towards Cardiff. The chart is lined with pencil marks of best intentions – a course to Peterstone Flats, beside Newport Deep.

It's lunchtime and the shaking waves of this morning are rounder now and less hurtful. But it would take a certain madness to venture too long into the galley, even in this swell. Sandwiches and crisps washed down with de-thawing coffee are on the menu.

This stretch of the Welsh coast could never be described as attractive. Its water is naturally brown and scraped from the muddied flats below its cliffs and siphoned from bulging rivers upstream. Its crowded coastline tells our industrial story; this is the business end of Wales – the workshop, the factory, the wharf of the industrial revolution. The story of Wales is all the more remarkable glimpsed from a yacht off its shores. Into this small concentration of coastline an empire was given the coal and iron of Wales. Without the toil of generations working beside the Ely, the Taff and the Rhymney, the world would have been a very different place.

Past Penarth and Cardiff Bay, Newport is close now: David sends me backwards down the ladder to the saloon to wind up the keel. Our next manoeuvre up a shallow river will require as little draught as possible. What feels like a hundred turns of the spanner lifts the plate which has saved us from drifting all morning.

The mouth of the river is marked by the West Usk and East Usk buoys, sentinels guarding a narrow and shallow channel. Last night's rain has washed the mountain's fragile earth into the Ebbw and the Usk and its course flows fast, clouded and brown. We sail slowly past the disused West Usk lighthouse, then beneath the pylons' stretched wires and under the bridge. All the time the depth meter falls, though high tide in an hour will give us enough time to tie up to explore the city.

The members of Uskmouth sailing club are a wonderful welcoming crowd. Like yacht clubs all over the country they know what the journey will have been like to even get to their jetty this afternoon. It takes us a second pass to tie up; the channel is full of moored boats and in a fast current trying to position *Swansong* is not easy.

David pretends to grovel and begs, 'Keep the shore leave to an hour, lads; it'll make life easier on the next leg.'

The ladies at the sailing club offer to cook a hot meal as we walk in. The colour of our skin must give our morning adventures away. It's almost rude to decline but there's no veering off plan.

David Hurn, the photographer who snapped The Beatles, Sean Connery, Jane Fonda, Clint Eastwood and most of the stars of the 1960s, is sitting at a table on the river bank in the centre of Newport, unrecognised by the shoppers milling around him. The man who made his name capturing the Hungarian Revolution for *TIME* magazine in 1956 is leafing through the papers. Since he set up the Documentary Photography School over the water from here he will have taught a good many news photographers. We've arranged to meet to talk about the huge change that his adopted city is undergoing.

David Hurn in the city of Newport

*'Steel Wave' by sculptor
Peter Fink*

He says he probably couldn't have chosen a better place in the country to teach reportage photography: Newport was experiencing great change then, as it is now, and the opportunity to capture a city, a country and a society at a moment when it was undergoing enormous upheaval was a wonderful privilege.

David breaks off for a moment and pulls a little camera out of his jacket to snap something that has caught his eye on the river bank. He's never off duty. David's later work has captured the changing face of Wales at the turn of the century. There is one particular photograph of his that sticks in my mind: 'Pouring at the steelworks', in Llanwern, epitomises a country desperately holding onto a proud industrial past, whilst fearing that another industrial revolution will consign its manufacturing to the history books.

'Come and look at our new bridge,' beckons David, getting up to walk along the river.

The wrappings are literally still on the clean new white paintwork of the Usk footbridge. This is the first part of the project to regenerate the centre of the city. Newport is having 'the waterside treatment' familiar to so many industrial cities that once used the tides to transport its treasures. They'll no doubt find new riches by developing the land overlooking the river.

David believes there is a sense of optimism here and renewal, but potential needs to be developed with taste. He looks down his lens, concerned but hopeful too that the city will make the right choices for the next chapter in its story.

In Newport's city centre, beautiful original shop-fronts peek out from the first floor but are masked at ground level by the hideous plastic façades of the chain stores. In front of them there's a modest statue to the man who wrote one of my favourite poems.

Because of the day's exertions rather than any over-whelming interest in poetry, the crew sit down in front of the statue for a breather. The good people of Newport sigh with the arrival of a few more scruffy-looking types.

W. H. Davies is known as the tramp poet and was born here in 1871. He left Britain for the USA in 1893 where he spent the next six years of his life working and begging across America. The turning point of his life was when he lost his leg in Ontario. He was dragged under the wheels of a train he tried to jump onto, as you do.

Unfit for manual labour, Davies turned to writing and returned to Britain where working-class verse was all the rage. At the age of fifty he married a prostitute thirty years his junior. The words carved into the stone go unread by the passing shoppers, too busy to read poetry today.

> What is this life if, full of care,
> We have no time to stand and stare?

SEVERN TUNNEL

It is hard today to imagine the River Severn without its two magnificent road crossings, or to imagine the hours of engineering and design skill which went into their construction. It is even harder, as we speed happily across in air-conditioned luxury, to remember that there's another crossing – a subterranean rail tunnel – hundreds of feet below us, beneath the river bed. For rail travellers from Paddington to south Wales, the Severn Tunnel, and its rival, the Severn Bridge, a railway crossing on stilts above the water (only finally demolished in 1970), were the wonders of the age. Even today, the tunnel still performs a magnificent job, cutting out the long trek around Gloucester and along the Severn estuary.

The building work began in March 1873 and progressed simultaneously at a number of points on both sides of the river. It involved the sinking of a series of shafts, including the quaintly named 5 Miles, 4 Chains. The entire operation was a battle against the elements as water constantly tried to force its way into the workings. When shafts and even the tunnel core itself were flooded, divers were employed in hazardous engineering missions, using pioneering techniques and equipment. In an age when workmen toiled by candlelight, it's amazing that the building of the tunnel, over 7,000 yards

in length, took only fourteen years. In that time whole villages grew up for the army of workpeople on both sides of the river, with a brickworks, hospital, school and even a Mission Hall. The Severn Tunnel was finally opened to passenger transport in December 1886.

Even today, in the well-lit comfort of a high-speed train, entering the tunnel is something of an adventure, with that strange feeling half-way through, that you are somehow moving backwards, whilst the occasional flash of brickwork reminds you that this engineering wonder is the work of human hands from another age.

Since Victorian times it isn't just goods and passengers which have travelled through the tunnel. Before the building of the road bridges, those motorists who chose not to use the ferry would wait at Severn Tunnel Junction to load their vehicles onto flat, open railcars. They then joined other rail passengers to make the short train journey through the tunnel, and were reunited with their cars at the other end, no doubt anxiously checking their paintwork to make sure no stray spark from the steam locomotive had caused any damage.

Top: to Aust, the ferry-point
Centre: Second Severn Crossing
Below: Severn bridge

Murals by Hans Feibusch

level drops and we must cast off with all speed to save getting stuck on the mud. The tide helps our passage out of the river Usk. There's a few hours sailing ahead and the gentle force speeding our departure downstream now will soon hinder our passage when we point the yacht up the Severn estuary later.

All sails aloft, the huge canvases block out the rays of the sun and the afternoon is drawing old. Past Portland Grounds, near Denny Island and the yacht groans and stiffens its sinews against the gathering force of the retreating tide. A freighter low in the water on the English side loiters off Avonmouth beneath the smoking towers.

I have driven over the river Severn hundreds of times but never sailed under its bridges. The passage of water at this stage of the tide is alarming to watch; a frothing wash of aggravated trouble. Throughout time man has battled with the simple question of how to cross this raging river. These two magnificent feats of engineering – the Severn Bridge and the Second Severn Crossing – are two giant landmarks. From a boat you can see how difficult their construction must have been. Our speed is now slowed and our progress determined by a current that is astonishing in strength.

The first and original Severn Bridge is the furthest one from us. I had always thought of it as simply a bridge – but from the water you can see it's a bridge connecting two viaducts sitting on the rocks. It consists not of one construction but three: the Aust viaduct, the Beachey viaduct and Wye bridge.

Our passage is becoming narrow now; we are sailing slowly up a deep central channel called 'The Shoots' bounded by some menacing rocks that will be

All of which elicits from cameraman Richard, 'Come on, we can't stand around here all day, we've only got half an hour left before we get back on the boat.'

We have been granted a rare treat to clamber to the top of Newport's civic buildings to film the city from one of its highest points. The quasi-Italianate style is very different from the other civic buildings of south Wales, and there's another surprise inside too. The building is home to some extraordinary murals painted by Hans Feibusch which depict Newport's history from the first Celtic settlement to the building of George Street Bridge. Who'd have thought you could take in a wonderful art exhibition while popping down the council offices? The climb up the clock tower is a marathon of steps, then ladders, and finally a spiral staircase opening onto the belfry where the hour is about to strike. You'll sneer if I say that the view from the top to the sea and to the hills was beautiful, won't you?

Back to the yacht and a pacing David, relieved that we're almost on time. With every minute, the river's

best avoided in low water. David, at the wheel, has been quiet for a while; this is taking all his concentration.

Above our heads is the massive humming concrete of the Second Severn Crossing carrying thousands of cars and trucks, oblivious to the little boat inching its way into its huge shadow. The daylight disappears for a moment and I can clearly see for the first time the frightening speed of the water passing the huge concrete buttresses beside us.

Daylight again and in the distance on the Welsh bank, visible through binoculars, I can just see the romantic and rather sad rusting hulk of the old Severn ferry boat. Resting above the high water line, it's forgotten and unloved, left behind in the slipstream of progress. It will take drivers no more than a minute to cross the river today, but for my parents' generation the journey over the water to England was far more of an adventure. In those days you were dependent on the timetable, weather conditions and there being enough

space on deck. There were three boats – *Severn Queen*, *Severn King* and *Severn Princess*. The last boat stopped the night before the bridge opened in 1966, and with its demise the experience of a voyage to another country ended.

'I can't risk letting you off,' says David, his first words for some time. 'It's just too rough today, the conditions are boisterous and the tide difficult. The crew will have to come back with me now.'

This was meant to be a one-way trip. We'd originally discussed jumping off somewhere on the Severn and rejoining the television crew following us on land for the return journey home. But all of us knew that somehow today's journey was always in the hands of the sea. She dictated our timetable from first light and our voyage will end on her terms too. It's four hours sailing back to Cardiff, and already the lights of evening are winking on the land. We are quiet once again and sit back in the cold air to watch the sea swallow the sun.

Severn Bridge, opened in 1966; Ferryboat now redundant

Leisure

WHAT is this life if, full of care,
We have no time to stand and stare?—

No time to stand beneath the boughs,
And stare as long as sheep and cows:

No time to see, when woods we pass,
Where squirrels hide their nuts in grass:

No time to see, in broad daylight,
Streams full of stars, like skies at night:

No time to turn at Beauty's glance,
And watch her feet, how they can dance:

No time to wait till her mouth can
Enrich that smile her eyes began?

A poor life this if, full of care,
We have no time to stand and stare.

W. H. Davies (1871-1940)

Herring gulls on Flat Holm

BORDER
COUNTRY

the company of one of the National Trust's staff. Sherie Soper, the castle's conservation officer, is our guide (and a musketeer with the Sealed Knot Society). I was half expecting to be sent around to the servants' entrance.

The castle is beautifully preserved. The visitors joining me on my tour range from camera-toting Japanese tourists to a middle-aged couple who are simply looking for something to do out of the rain.

Chirk Castle has been continuously occupied for almost seven centuries. The descendants of Sir Thomas Myddelton, who bought the place for £5,000 in 1595, still live here. Even on a rainy day the windows offer breathtaking views of the parkland across to the Ceiriog valley. The castle was thought to have been built by Roger Mortimer who was granted the area by Edward I after the Welsh defeat in 1282. The fourteenth-century structure is preserved in the Adam's tower which has an enormous dungeon on two floors shrouded by five-metre-thick walls. This construction could withstand nuclear war, let alone cannon fire.

Elizabeth I granted the castle to her favourite, Robert Dudley, Earl of Leicester and Baron of Denbigh. Chirk's next owner was no less notable; Sir Thomas Myddelton was the founder of the East India Company, and a stakeholder in the expeditions of Drake and Raleigh. It was Myddelton who began the process of changing the castle from a stronghold into a comfortable Tudor home.

Our guide, Sherie, leads her small, damp party to the Cromwell Hall, which is festooned with every manner of weapon imaginable. She takes down an ancient musket from the wall and demonstrates how it would have been loaded, positioned and then fired. It suddenly strikes me how strange it is to see a woman holding a gun.

Castle gardens

'It's a little-known fact that women fought in the Civil War and would have used weapons like this to great effect,' Sherie tells the gathering who slowly begin to edge away. The Japanese tourists look on rather nervously and decide not to ask any more questions until she's put the gun down.

In the Long Room, the centre of attention is an ornate ebony cabinet full of secret drawers, a gift from Charles II to Myddelton for his support. I prefer the kind of cronyism that rewards patronage with a cabinet for your place, rather than a place in the cabinet.

Sherie is a borderer, from Oswestry. When I ask her about the characteristics of the people who live around here she agrees that she and her family would think of themselves as borderers, and that they do have distinct characteristics – tending to be pragmatic and able to get along with both sides. In this case, getting along well with the Welsh as well as the English, although first remembering to take stock of which way the wind is blowing. It's no surprise, therefore, that the castle changed sides in the Civil War.

On Wednesdays the countryside came into town, drowning it out with the distinctive Welsh of Powys. Every shopkeeper who could speak a little of the old language dusted it down every Wednesday, and every Thursday put it away again. Groups of farmers and their wives stood here and there, discussing the land, the weather and the price of eggs. It's warm or it's cold, we need rain or a dry spell, the heifers are dear or cheap, and someone's died or married or made a terrible mess of things. The same conversation from one group to the next, with only the names changed . . . Shrill-voiced farmers from up-country pulling one another's legs in a torrent of Welsh, and sullen men from the lowlands talking drab sense in atrocious English.

Islwyn Ffowc Elis (1924-2004), *Shadow of the Sickle* (trans. Meic Stephens)

Jim Saunders

Oswestry, on which Islwyn Ffowc Elis based the fictional town of Henberth

Above: Chirk parkland; below: Pontcysyllte aqueduct

Outside the castle, the day has dried up and the grounds look like they've been scrubbed up for the afternoon. Clipped yews, roses and climbers soften the harsh walls around the formal garden. A thatched 'Hawk House', a rock garden and shrub garden with its small pool and rare trees are invitingly seductive. Offa's Dyke runs through the park. It's interesting to see where previous improvers have simply moved the dyke or flattened it to make way for the bold new designs of landscape gardeners. No sense of reverence for the past stopped demolition of what we would now call an ancient monument; nothing got in the way of the Myddelton makeover of Chirk Castle or its grounds. Conservation is a twentieth-century notion.

A wedding party gathers at the gates; it's all part of the business of keeping a stately home running. Where once the marauding masses would have had hot oil poured on their heads, they are now welcomed with open arms to spend their money to help Chirk keep up appearances. Next to the morning suits, I feel under-dressed in my waterproofs; time to find Aled and get back on our bikes.

It's a short ride and mostly downhill from the castle's squat seat to the aqueduct already busy with narrow boats taking advantage of the belated appearance of the sun. There's not really enough room on the tow path for us to cycle side by side but despite the director's best efforts, we don't actually oblige him with his perfect shot – though falling into the canal wouldn't make either of us much wetter now. The aqueduct was built two hundred years ago by Thomas Telford. Fifty years later it was joined by its close neighbour the viaduct, purposefully built higher, they

say, so that the new train passengers could look down smugly from their carriages and see the old canal below. Those boaters who are tanned from a fortnight's holiday look wonderfully relaxed for having pootled not very far at an average of four miles per hour. It's a perfect metaphor for our times: a once-abandoned, grimy industrial network has been reclaimed for the pursuit of pleasure and leisure. This stretch can even claim a Hollywood star's recent holiday endorsement.

The view of the Ceiriog valley from the middle of the aqueduct back through the viaduct's arches is awesome.

Our route back into Oswestry takes us alongside the shimmering canal, flashing sunlight and where the tow path is bursting with flowers and shrubs.

The morning's rain, my still sodden clothes and more vigorous pedalling than expected have all conspired to produce a good deal of chafing and considerable exhaustion. I'm looking forward to a break from cycling, sitting down and drying off.

In the still air of early evening the strains of Sir Henry Walford Davies's 'RAF March Past' drift out of Christ Church, Oswestry – it's band practice night for Porthywaen Silver Band. The band was set up in the 1930s and draws its members from both sides of Offa's Dyke. They're a healthy gathering of young and old members, a successful bunch who've even performed at the Royal Albert Hall. There's a certain poignancy in hearing the 'RAF March Past' rehearsed here. This was the composer's family church; both he and his brothers played the organ at services.

It really is a delight to sit in the pews at the back of the church in Arthur Street and listen to this work

Porthywaun Silver Band at Christ Church, Oswestry

The magnificent ironwork gates and gate-screens which form the entrance to the parkland of the Chirk estate are known locally as the Pretty Gates, and rightly so. The wrought-iron tracery in baroque fashion is an outstanding feature of Chirk and many visitors come to see the gates as works of art in themselves.

They were made by two brothers, Robert and John Davies, at Croesfoel Forge, Bersham, just outside Wrexham, and are dated 1719. They bear the coat-of-arms of the Myddelton family and also the 'Red Hand of Chirk' at the top. The three wolves and the eagle from the coat-of-arms appear again in the patterns on the gate and on the pallisade. The story explaining the red hand's significance is a rather chilling one. There was an inheritance dispute, apparently, in the very distant past, and two sons decided to race in order to win the title of Lord of Chirk and the estate itself. When the winning man was about to reach out for the finish (the walls of the castle, or, in another version, the far bank of the lake, after a swimming race), a friend of his brother lashed out with a sword and cut off his hand. Not surprisingly, the unharmed man won the race.

The gates seem exceptionally grand for their position, nearly two kilometres from the castle itself. But they were originally on the forecourt of the castle, between flanking walls. They were moved in 1770 when major landscaping took place in the parkland, and then moved again in 1888 to their present position.

The gates were originally white but were painted black during the Second World War and were not restored to their former glory until the beginning of the twenty-first century. The cost of caring for such a large-scale work of art is considerable: in 1998 the cost of repairs required was estimated at £191,000.

Interestingly an iron mask which used to hang on the gates was sold at auction in 2004, along with several other items from the Chirk estate.

played time and again. This evening, the master of the music is the conductor David Thomas from Rhosllannerchrugog.

Walford Davies was born in Oswestry. He went on to become a composer, teacher, organist and Britain's first classical-music radio personality. In 1918, he was appointed the RAF's Director of Music, where he wrote perhaps his best known work, the 'RAF March Past', a piece that has accompanied most ceremonial military events ever since. A year later, Davies was appointed Professor of Music at Aberystwyth. Here he championed the cause of Welsh composers and musicians for the next twenty years.

The young organist who learnt his music in this church won the hearts of radio listeners across Britain with his series of wireless talks which began in 1926 and lasted until the outbreak of war in 1939. Following Elgar's death, Davies was appointed Master of the King's Musick. The congregation who once worshipped at Christ Church must have watched with pride and delight at the success of the little boy whom they had taken to their hearts and helped educate when Davies's father died suddenly in 1885. The people of Oswestry set up a memorial fund to look after Walford Davies and his brothers. It was generosity that he would never forget.

Outside the stained-glass windows, the light is slipping away and I have an appointment with a medieval nun before sunset.

I'm not usually a fan of dressing up in period costume, particularly when it involves walking the streets of a British market town on a Saturday night. Sue Ellis dresses up every day for visitors to Oswestry

The band with conductor David Thomas; Sue Ellis

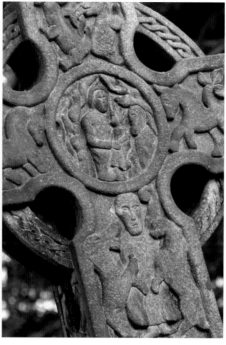

In pilgrim garb; Celtic cross in the Parish churchyard, not quite street pedlars

who come to explore the town's history. When she opens the door in her full pilgrimage outfit, it's hard to refuse her persuasive attempts to enter into the spirit of her daily missionary work.

Saturday in Oswestry is the same as it is everywhere else in Britain – a wind-down boozy affair with a hint of good-natured menace. As I slip into a medieval costume with a black hood, the crew look away to save laughing in company. Just imagine the BBC paperwork if we get beaten up. 'Whilst walking the streets of Oswestry in the company of a nun, dressed as a medieval pilgrim . . .'

Sue in full regalia doesn't bat an eyelid as we walk past a crowd of gawping teenagers and begins her well-practised night-time tour of Ancient Oswestry. I look like a cross between an Islamic preacher and the Vicar of Dibley and try not to trip over my oversized smock. Judging by the whiff, it may have been medieval times since this get-up last had a good wash.

Most of the town centre is a conservation area and a mish-mash of old timbered houses. The Blackgate, the Fox Inn and the shops along Beatrice Street are well-preserved, and for a moment Sue and I look more in keeping with our surroundings than the tracksuit wearers stopping to stare at us. There are some splendid Georgian town houses around St Oswald's Church and the Victorians, too, have left a legacy of shop fronts, beautiful terraced houses and railway buildings.

A historical tour of Oswestry with Sue brings the story of the town alive in a way that no book ever could. Moreover, her enthusiastic legends are delivered at breakneck walking speed.

Oswestry Castle dates from around 1086 and is mentioned in the Domesday Book. It was once a frontier outpost that saw the Welsh and Anglo Saxons mix together well before the Norman Conquest. The earliest reference to the town itself is in 1272 and the settlement of Blancminster, whose name derives from the white stone church.

I'm trying to look intelligent at this point whilst peering out of my black hoodie.

The Welsh refer to a Croes Oswallt in 1254, an obvious link with King Oswald killed up the road in 641. Regardless of paucity of written historical evidence, it's generally accepted that Oswestry was once a strong Welsh settlement and that the town's castle was built to subdue Welsh resistance.

A small crowd is gathering around us and some of them are even listening to Sue. Now I know what it feels like to be stared at by crowds, like the lions in a zoo.

The occupation of the castle by Madog ap Maredudd, Prince of Powys between 1149 and 1157, was one of a number of changes of nationality during Oswestry's turbulent history. On this occasion it was the chance to reclaim what the Welsh had lost.

Two rather unsteady men who have clearly been drinking all afternoon wobble across the road to take a closer look at us in our costumes but quickly retreat when they realise we are not all that they had hoped.

In the fourteenth century, Owain Glyndŵr attempted to establish himself as the rightful Prince of Wales and during this period Oswestry blossomed as an important trading town. A friend of Glyndŵr's, David Holbache, established the town's school in 1407 – the earliest secular foundation in Britain except for Winchester.

Oswestry Grammar School, now the Heritage Centre; Llwyd Mansion, built in 1604

OFFA'S DYKE

Above: with archaeologist Margaret Worthington; right: Offa's Dyke at Discoed

Offa's Dyke is around twelve hundred years old and is Britain's longest archaeological monument. It is 129 km long, with 64 km in Wales and 65 km in England. It stretches (with some gaps) from Sedbury Cliffs on the Severn estuary (in southern Gloucestershire) to Treuddyn, near Wrexham, in north-east Wales. Typically, it consists of a bank up to eight metres high with a ditch on its western side, but today this shape is visible in only a few well-protected areas. It is an amazing feat of engineering, especially when one remembers that only hand tools would have been available to the workforce. Nothing on this scale was subsequently built in Britain until a thousand years later, with the construction of the Trent and Mersey Canal.

The dyke was built by King Offa, sovereign of the Anglo-Saxon kingdom of Mercia from 757-796 AD. Mercia covered the modern English midlands and beyond, and was the most powerful of the separate kingdoms which existed in Britain at this time. Offa, like all kings of his time, was a warrior as well as a statesman, and fought at least three military campaigns in a what is now Wales. He was a ruthless politician, seizing power by force, and is known to have murdered rivals such as King Aethelbert of East Anglia.

It is not easy to determine why an earthwork on this scale was commissioned. It may have had military uses, being a good vantage point from which to keep an eye on the Welsh, or it may have been chiefly a symbol of power and status. It may even have acted as a frontier for trade, allowing people and goods to pass to and fro.

From the Offa's Dyke Path, which is a National Trail, walkers are able to follow considerable stretches of the dyke and observe it from other parts of the trail. When the path was opened in 1971, a decision was taken to take the trail north of Llangollen westward onto the Clwydian Hills, rather than east, to follow the earthwork through the suburbs of Wrexham. That is why the path ends in the north not on the dyke itself, confusingly, but in Prestatyn.

It's getting late now and after two hours of walking very fast (or at least fast enough to shake off the curious and a couple of stray dogs) it's the end of our historical tour of Oswestry.

The first rule of being a medieval pilgrim with a nun in tow is, when walking the streets in a strange town, dump the fancy dress before it gets too dark. The bar of the Wynnstay Hotel beckons, then for me it's dinner and bed.

In the best traditions of hedging their bets, the weathermen have promised another day of sunshine and showers. Aled arrives early with the mountain bikes in the back of his van and joins us for an early breakfast. He says he remembers being taken to the market here when he was a little boy and hearing as much Welsh spoken amongst the stalls as English, but that is beginning to change now.

Our plan is to cycle as close as possible to Offa's Dyke today. The roads around Trefonnen are still empty. No one rises this early on Sunday, particularly on a day that's so wet.

We've come here to meet one of the world's most interesting photographers. Ben Osbourne is squatting in a stream by the side of the road photographing raindrops hitting the surface of the water. If you've ever seen any of David Attenborough's wildlife films, Ben is the photographer who produces those beautiful books that accompany the series. He specialises in wildlife and landscape photography ranging from oil spills to rain forests. His book *Life in the Freezer* documents the period he spent living in Antarctica so it's perhaps best not to whinge about the weather today. His other celebrated work, *Blue Planet*, explored

Ben Osborne

the world's oceans, so interviewing him in the rain shouldn't trouble him unduly. The man who rows for days along Africa's rivers to discover a lost tribe or a rare bird or animal comes home to the Welsh Borders.

'I've travelled the length of Offa's Dyke and there is something intriguing about the differing characteristics of the landscape and the people on either side of the border,' he tells me. 'I think it's the difference between the highland life of Wales and its culture and the flatter lowlands of the English side. The geographical contrast between the two countries is so clearly visible, but the people are different too. It just takes time to discover.'

We leave Ben in the stream. He's admittedly a rather odd sight – up to his knees in water, bending over earnestly, photographing raindrops. But his act of worship this Sunday will result in the most wonderful pictures and he's been fascinating company.

A half-mile cycle ride down the road, the staff at the Barley Mow pub are getting ready for their lunchtime service as well: crates out, glasses polished, food unwrapped and tables wiped. The hordes requiring Sunday lunch will arrive in a few hours. Our

At the Barley Mow pub and brewery

interest is in an early lunch, I admit, but the pub is built into Offa's Dyke, and from here we will later pick up the trail of the ancient monument for a few miles.

Proprietor Shane Parr's ancestors were deported to Australia for brewing illicit liquor so it's a delightful twist of history that that he has returned from Australia to the Welsh border to brew beer on Offa's Dyke. His brewery is a little barn next door to the pub and he invites us all in, after donning the necessary protective clothes, to smell the hops and see the still.

Everyone is pretty worn down after a morning's damp filming. The invitation to 'try a beer' doesn't need to be repeated.

After a few midday pints, Shane divulges his difficulties in trying to name his new brew. 'Offa's Beer' sounds like a special discount and 'Dyke's Beer' sounds like the last question before a fight. It's not easy being a brewer.

Outside it's *still* raining. There couldn't be a worse day for the Trefonnen Scarecrow Festival on the village green. The children (but mostly the adults) of the village have turned out for the midday start of the

event. The ground is like a bog and the smaller infants have long disappeared into the quagmire. Today they will have to introduce a special category for 'Best Trench Foot' for the scarecrow who most bravely survives another torrential downpour. Anyway, regardless of families being swept away in the flood, at Trefonnen they are determined to carry on.

I'm so wet now there's no point sheltering from the rain. As in so many other places, farming is a declining industry here. It's highly mechanised, and employs very few people. Most of the people here work in offices; they have no crops to look after. Yet for all that there is something deep within these people urging them to come and make a scarecrow. Admittedly it's fun for the kids, but I think there is also something else at play – a desire to reconnect with nature and to reach back to another age.

A few miles down the road in Treflach, we are met by Margaret Worthington, an archaeologist who has spent years excavating sites around Offa's Dyke.

'So where is it, Margaret?' I ask, searching the horizon hazy with lifting clouds. After all this build-up, I'm finally looking forward to seeing Offa's Dyke up close at last.

'You're standing on it,' she replies, a little breathless and now looking as crestfallen as I feel.

In his classic travel book, *Wild Wales*, George Borrow says that it was customary for the English to cut off the ears of every Welshman who was found to the east of the dyke, and for the Welsh to hang every Englishman whom they found to the west of it.

Offa's Dyke may have been a potent symbol of the antipathy between England and Wales since it was built in the eighth century but like an unloved, elderly dog, it has been ignored, ruined and contemptuously destroyed in many places. I don't know what I was expecting – perhaps that this ancient monument would look more cared for. On this stretch, it's simply an overgrown shallow ditch and a hedge-sized mound.

'There is so much of it, that the prevailing view used to be that it mattered little if it was moved, removed or damaged further,' says Margaret wistfully.

Offa's Dyke is as important to the story of Wales as Hadrian's Wall is to Scotland but it surely needs to be rescued and revered.

The sun's coming out for the last hours of the afternoon. Past Llanymynech and Llantrinio, after a brisk pedal we arrive in Criggion. It probably won't mean anything to you, but this little enclave tucked inside the Welsh border was once one of Britain's last lines of defence during both the Second World War and the Cold War. Criggion's huge hill, a thousand feet above the valley floor, provided pioneering wireless engineers with the necessary water supply from the river Severn to cool their equipment and sufficient height to hang a large aerial. If Britain's main wartime transmitter at Rugby was bombed then Criggion was the standby station for radio communications. The ships engaged in the pursuit of the Bismarck were helped with the messages received and sent from this base and Criggion's assistance in eavesdropping in the Cold War was no less significant. Who'd have thought that in this quiet backwater so far from anywhere you'd find an essential nerve centre for wartime communications?

We leave the bikes at the entrance and wander around the deserted and derelict rooms which are wide

open to the world. Wires hang from the ceilings and walls in what looks like an exploded spaghetti factory. This is a part of the history of Wales that has no guide book or visitor centre. The work that was carried out here is still shrouded in secrecy.

As we turn to leave, I can't help thinking about those young technical geniuses who worked here during the darkest hours of the Second World War and the Cold War. They must have walked over the same land and shared the same thoughts as those who built and sheltered behind Offa's Dyke. Two generations who shared a fear of war, and perhaps hoped their endeavours would bring an end to uncertainty. Two generations stationed right here, sharing the experience of conflict but separated by hundreds of years.

I told you there was something intriguing about borders.

Left above: at Criggion;
Trefonnen Scarecrow
Festival

After asking a few questions as to the road we were to take, we left the house, and in a little time entered the valley of Ceiriog. The valley is very narrow, huge hills overhanging it on both sides, those on the east side lumpy and bare, those on the west precipitous, and partially clad with wood; the torrent Ceiriog runs down it, clinging to the east side; the road is tolerably good, and is to the west of the stream. Shortly after we had entered the gorge, we passed by a small farm-house on our right hand, with a hawthorn hedge before it, upon which seems to stand a peacock, curiously cut out of thorn. Passing on we came to a place called Pandy uchaf, or the higher Fulling mill. The place so called is a collection of ruinous houses, which put me in mind of the Fulling mills mentioned in Don Quixote. It is called the Pandy because there was formerly a fulling mill here, said to have been the first established in Wales.

George Borrow (1803-1881) *Wild Wales*

Ceiriog valley

PRESELI

Aled Hughes

HILL COUNTRY ON HORSEBACK

There is a sense of separateness about north Pembrokeshire – it is unconquered, undiluted and unspoiled. It was a regular family picnic destination when we were kids, with grandparents often in

Carn Menyn (Meini)

tow. It seemed then to be a marathon journey with enough equipment to climb Everest: rugs, folding chairs, parasol for Gran and an overflowing picnic basket.

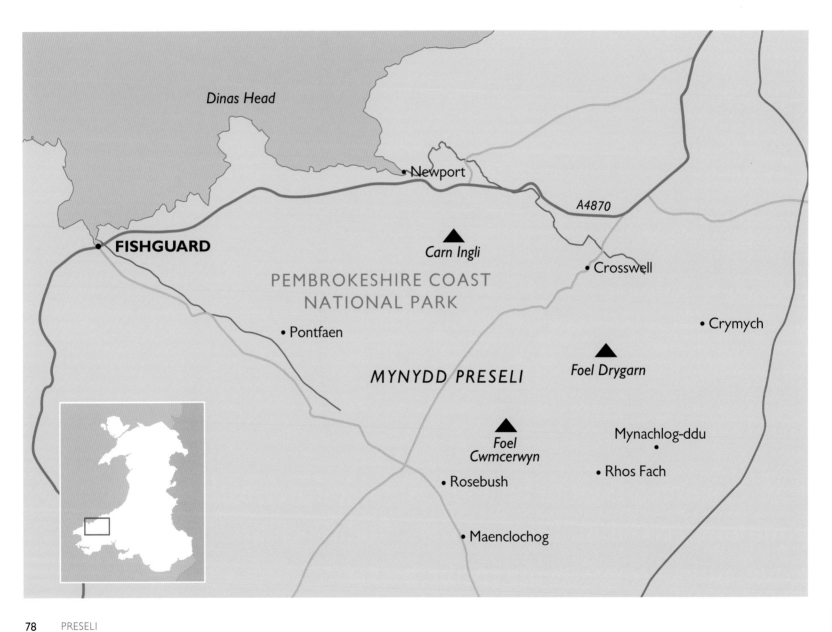

THERE IS A CERTAIN FOLLY IN ATTEMPTING to ride across the Preseli Hills on horseback. For a start, I haven't really ridden a horse since I was a child, and moreover, the presence of a camera crew to record the event will unnerve the animal and commit my mistakes to the immortal archives.

We were sent for horse-riding lessons when we were kids growing up on the other side of the county from here. Sunday mornings led by Paddy Dowson were a ruse of my parents to reclaim their peace at the weekends. Our routes were the quiet, empty backstreets of Pembroke Dock, perhaps to the graveyard where Dad is now buried. It wasn't especially beautiful but it was a journey without our parents nonetheless, which at the age of five or six was exciting enough. Apart from that time, and the later ownership of a pony called Jill, who went the way of the family's white rabbits, I can't really claim to have had the experience that makes an accomplished horseman. My teenage nieces, who are both competent riders, have warned me that my adventure in the Preseli Hills will leave me with a sore backside.

So I find myself walking into Crosswell Riding Stables and the prospect of two days in the saddle. Carolyn Morgan has been leading and teaching the nervous and the incompetent for twenty years. She has the perfect combination of patience, a love of animals and people to put me at my ease, at least until I climb onto the horse. She knows the bridleways of these hills with her eyes closed. But my Preseli expedition doesn't start quite yet. First, there is a morning at the sand school. The tack-room reeks of old leather, and from its walls, lines of bridles, ropes and saddles hang. Beneath,

Lesson at the sand school

a box of a few dozen riding hats that look like swollen black footballs, and beside them, neat rows of riding boots, polished and shining. The brown leather display gives onto a garish line of red, yellow and blue rosettes for four-legged triumphs at horse-shows throughout Pembrokeshire. Sellotaped to the window are the parish notices of the equestrian world: a bric-a-brac sale for the pony club in Crymych, and notice of the next meeting of Tivyside Hunt. It's a year since Britain's politicians in Westminster banned hunting but, in Pembrokeshire, the new law continues to be interpreted as local people see fit.

Squeezed into a borrowed riding hat, boots and chaps, I wander over to the stable to be introduced to Blue, who doesn't look up from chewing his straw. This is rather like a blind date: neither of us knows each other, but will spend the next two days hopefully inseparable . . . at least that's what I'm hoping for from our new relationship. I tell Carolyn that I'm praying for the Morris Oxford of the horse fraternity – something very slow that doesn't go around corners too fast. She says

Pembrokeshire lanes

that her animals can suss out their riders immediately. If that is true, then Blue will know that he's going to be mounted by the equine equivalent of a learner driver who's about to crucify the gearbox. Actually, the sound of crunching gears would have been preferable to the noise that accompanied the rest of the morning.

When you've only known someone for a few minutes, there's a certain embarrassment in dealing with the sound of breaking wind. If you've never been in earshot of a horse breaking wind, believe me, it can be a force of remarkable velocity. As we pace around the sand school, Carolyn's shouted instructions from the end of a long rope are accompanied by what sounds like the brass section of an orchestra. On my journey across the Preseli Hills, I'll be travelling with a horse that cannot stop farting.

Sounds apart, as we walk out of the yard at Crosswell and into its tree-tunnelled lanes, the scenery is mesmerising. Although I come from Pembrokeshire, I can't claim to know this part of the county well. If you grew up in the south, the north was another country. Rather like a miniature of Wales, south Pembrokeshire is anglicised and there is little Welsh spoken, but the north is heartland Welsh-speaking country. The south, especially the Milford Haven area, is heavily industrialised, its skies poked by the oil industry, whereas the north is still for the most part rural farming country. Older inhabitants still refer to the inhabitants of the south as 'the down belows' (as though labelling the genitalia of a newly-discovered, but ugly anatomical specimen).

When I turned seventeen, my grandfather taught me to drive in his wheezing Morris Minor and we came here to escape the main roads and get lost in the sign-less lanes that beguile strangers. I still get lost when I drive here, so perhaps it's time to get the upper hand.

I have to admit, even though it galls me, the first few hours astride Blue are spent riding very, very gingerly. Soon the rhythmic clip-clopping becomes like a metronome keeping time on our travels.

The great thing about being up this high and moving so slowly is you can see over hedges and into gardens. If you were to do this from a big car, the intrusion of privacy would be viewed with hostility, but it's difficult not to smile at a horse gawping through your window, particularly when its rider is clinging on for dear life.

The Preseli Hills are dotted with prehistoric remains – this is one of the landscapes of Britain that modern man has done relatively little to tame. Some historians maintain the so-called bluestones from these hills were transported to construct the inner circle and horseshoe of Stonehenge. But as our animals amble onwards, side by side, Carolyn and I agree we've never met a builder who didn't take the easy way out, and that Ice Age glaciers doing the hard work is the more plausible explanation.

The lanes leading from the stables are narrowing by the week – alternating days of gentle rain and sun have drawn a sea of bluebells from the earth. Above them, the trees are in early full canopy, offering gentle shade from this morning's promised sun. Carolyn and I ride close together. I assume this is so we can talk without shouting, and then it dawns on me that, at a stroke, she can grab my reins if she needs to. At first, I feel a growing impatience to trot faster, the pace of the working week

Above: Y Frenni Fawr and Foel Drygarn from Crosswell, our starting point; below: near the summit of Foel Cwmcerwyn

Moorland heather

still coursing through my veins, but within an hour, I begin to realise why horse-riders always smile when you pass them – they have discovered the ecstasy of slowing down your life. I can feel myself unwinding and drinking in the fields on either side. There seems something missing from all this, and then I realise we haven't passed a car for ages; I've ridden back into the 1950s.

I watch Carolyn as she draws ahead of me. She sits on her horse as though she is part of it, they move as one, whereas any casual observer will see the sack of potatoes astride Blue has some way to go before that synchronicity is reached.

A mile outside Crosswell, and we are onto the wild heathland of the lower slopes of Mynydd Preseli. Carolyn's horse needs no further encouragement than rough grass beneath the hooves – the turbo is switched on, and it's clear these two animals would ordinarily be racing up the hill were it not for the awkward bloke hanging onto Blue.

Stretched out before us are the rising slopes of the Preseli 'Mountains' – as we 'down belows' know them in our low-lying part of the county. But these are actually the gentle hills of Pembrokeshire, kinder than the higher mountains of the Brecon Beacons or Snowdonia's crueller peaks. This is the home of the legend of the Mabinogion where Arthur and his knights crossed the ridge and fought the Twrch Trwyth – the magic boar – on the slopes of Foel Cwmcerwyn. I'm hoping that the boar has long gone because my horsemanship skills do not yet run to galloping.

The metallic clops on tarmac are replaced now with subdued thuds on grass, and off the road's hard surface the only sound to be heard are the distant flocks of

Dyfed Elis-Gruffydd

Aled Hughes

calling sheep as we begin to climb the slopes near Foel Drygarn. The horses instinctively know that beneath the yellowed green of the moorland, there are springs and spongy ground, treacherous for misplaced hooves, so they daintily climb, finding their own route.

High on the hill, frowning down on us, are the remains of an ancient fort, two rings of stonework astride its top, and a double ditch to discourage intruders and learner riders. At first, the piles of stones seem like discarded debris from careless Iron Age masons – but these are the earlier Bronze Age burial cairns that give Foel Drygarn its Welsh name: Hill of Three Cairns. This ancient place would have been chosen for settlement and grazing of animals because all the land lower down the slope would have been thick forest.

Blue's ears twitch periodically like radar; he's seen a few baby rabbits in a gorse bush beside Carolyn, but senses that chasing after them would unseat me. We're slowly coming to an understanding: he understands I'm not very good and he's taking it nice and gently. The mountain is quite empty – save for a million filthy sheep. It's early in the season and the birdwatchers, walkers and holidaymakers won't come in numbers for several weeks yet. The hills are ours, bleak and stunning.

Mynachlog-ddu is an hour's ride away, and the need to fill awkward silences in conversation between strangers has passed. Carolyn leads the way and seems more confident now about my horsemanship, which is a triumph for me, albeit a small one.

Foel Dygarn; Gorse on Rhos Fach

The chiefest and principal mountain of this shire is Presely, which is a long ridge or rank of mountains running east and west, beginning above Pencelli Fawr, where the first mount of high land thereof is called Moel Eryr, and so passing eastward to Cwm Cerwyn, being the highest part of it, runs east to Moel Trygarn and to Llanfyrnach. This mountain is about six or seven miles long and two miles broad. It has in it many hills rising in the high mountain, which are to be discerned twenty miles, thirty miles, forty miles off, and more, and from this hill may be seen all Pembrokeshire and some parts of nine other shires . . . The commodity of this mountain is great, for it yields plenty of good grass and is full of sweet springs of water. It yields also store of fuel for the inhabitants adjoining, for most of the mountain yields good peat and turf . . .

The Description of Pembrokeshire by George Owen of Henllys, written *c*.1603

Capel Bethel, Mynachlog-ddu; the grave of Thomas Rees, Twm Carnabwth

The ride to the village takes us past dense forestry and wide, steep moorland. In Mynachlog-ddu it's still early on Saturday; still too cold for brunch outdoors, but from Blue's saddle, I can see several well-spread tables in the kitchens of cottages as we clop back onto the road. An old man stands in his front doorway; flat cap on, just staring, watching, the way old Welshmen do.

Bethel chapel cemetery is well kept and the grass freshly mown. After a few hours in the saddle, I could do with getting off for a few minutes. If I'm honest, I haven't quite mastered the correct rhythm for cantering yet, and the last stretch has left me feeling as though I've just been kicked in the crotch. Carolyn's just getting into the swing of a long day's ride and holds Blue's reins as I leap unsteadily onto the earth-bank boundary of the graveyard, grateful for a moment to stand up and stretch my legs. Carolyn stays in the saddle.

The stone-fronted chapel is newly-painted and looked after with pride. On a new grave there are fresh flowers in a jam jar resting on the brown earth; it's still too early for a headstone to be carved. In the corner beside the back of the chapel, beyond leaning memorials, is the final resting-place of one of Pembrokeshire's most colourful sons. Twm Carnabwth is buried here; he's said to have been a prominent figure in the Rebecca Riots in the 1830s. Local people were incensed about the imposition of road taxes at toll-gates. Twm, legend has it, had a reputation as a bit of a drinker and was fond of fighting. A large man, he would appear as a prizefighter at nearby fairs, and was the perfect chap to lead an uprising of the disgruntled. In 1847, he lost an eye in a drunken brawl.

There is something undeniably romantic about the Rebecca Riots – however unromantic the conditions under which the ordinary people of south and west Wales laboured in the early years of the nineteenth century. Writers and filmmakers alike, from Alexander Cordell to Dylan Thomas (who wrote the original screenplay for *Rebecca's Daughters*) have responded to the rioters' heady combination of danger, drama and working-class heroism.

Although unjust taxation and poor living and working conditions contributed to the common people's unhappiness, it was the injustice of the toll-gate system which really infuriated the rioters, daughters of Rebecca as they became known. Eleven different turnpike companies operated in Carmarthenshire alone and it became impossible for a tenant-farmer to move stock or even transport lime to fertilize his fields, without paying a small fortune in levies and charges. And so the attacks upon the toll-gates began, each assault led by a 'mother' and her 'daughters', men dressed in women's clothes, with faces blackened to prevent recognition. The reason for the choice of the name Rebecca is arguable: some say that Twm Carnabwth, Thomas Rees, borrowed the clothes of his neighbour Rebecca; others believe that the name was suggested by the verse from Genesis: *And they blessed Rebekah, and said unto her, Thou art our sister, be thou the mother of thousands of millions, and let thy seed possess the gate of those which hate them.*

Even today the border area between Pembrokeshire and Carmarthenshire, where much of the rioting took place, is called *Bro Beca* (Rebecca's neighbourhood) and it is a testament to the courage and determination of the campaigners that their activities are remembered as one of the highpoints of Welsh history.

Photographs: Aled Hughes

Dyfed Elis-Gruffydd

Slopes of Talmynydd; memorial stone to Waldo Williams

In later years, Twm Carnabwth changed his ways and became a respected lay preacher. According to the verse on his gravestone he died tending cabbages in his garden, though his death certificate says asthma was the cause of his passing, which doesn't paint such an idyllic picture. For me, the legendary status which Twm Carnabwth has in these parts typifies a certain west Walian spirit of dissent and political nonconformism that is still prevalent in north Pembrokeshire today; this is the wild west, a long way from the city.

And now I'm delaying the moment that you've been waiting for, when I attempt to mount Blue again, except this time, there won't be a handy mounting block like the one in the stable-yard. Well, you can wipe that expectant smile off your face, as the chapel bank allows me to get my leg over with the greatest of ease. The camera crew look disappointed too.

In Mynachlog-ddu, the trickles of water in Tewgyll Fach and Afon Tewgyll pass us in the opposite direction on their way to Afon Cleddau Ddu or Eastern Cleddau. The road is framed by ancient, moss-covered stone walls keeping back a flourishing crop of wild garlic, pungent and damp from this morning's early rain. On Rhos Fach, a standing stone commemorates the life of Waldo Williams, poet and pacifist, who went to school in Mynachlog-ddu. His work is much-revered and has been translated into several languages – including English by the Archbishop of Canterbury, Rowan Williams.

Our route leads along the edge of Craig Talfynydd to the standing stones beside Glynsaithmaen farm. Its buildings are squat; the barns, piggery and house look as though they've grown from the mountain's stone. A pack of dogs startle the horses for a moment, and I realise that if Blue bolts now, I won't know what to do except hold on for dear life. And then comes a shout from inside the house, at which the dogs immediately switch from wild to cowering. They are admonished and slink back to their lair.

A slight man walks purposefully across the yard, wiping his mouth. Len Jones is in his seventies but is as thin and wiry as a teenager. His face is red from the cold and the wind, and although it is the middle of a warm day, he wears a hat that completely covers his head and his ears.

Len announces he's in the middle of his dinner, and he won't be with us for a short while. This is a wonderful moment: camera crews the world over are used to interviewees dropping everything to be filmed for the telly, and a wide smile breaks out among the crew. It's lunchtime at Glynsaithmaen farm and it will take more than the BBC to disturb the order of the day.

Carolyn and I let the horses saunter around the

yard. It was in these barns that the first Rebecca Rioters are said to have met before attacking the toll-gate at Efailwen in 1839. These days the conspirators' rendezvous is home to an ancient Ferguson tractor and a dozen startled hens. The yard looks like a museum of a hundred years of agricultural machinery. Farmers never throw out old equipment in case it might one day come in handy.

Len walks briskly, straight-backed, across the yard. He's worked as a shepherd for over fifty years in the Preseli Hills, which is remarkable enough, but he's one of the few shepherds who still tends his flock from horseback, which makes him pretty well unique. Many farms shepherd their sheep from a quad bike or a 4 x 4. We are about to witness living history.

Len shouts in Welsh to his invisible dogs and they appear immediately in stealthy silence. Blue is unnerved for a moment and then settles. Len saddles up his horse, Rock, watched intently by Carolyn who knows an expert horseman when she sees one. I know she's interested in obtaining Rock's services as a stud for one of her mares. No command is necessary for Len's animal to move off; they have a long mutual respect and understanding that has no need of words.

Len leads Carolyn and me and an entourage of dogs through the cobbled yard, past the farmhouse and onto rough pasture in the shadow of Foel Cwmcerwyn. With the three of us in line I feel as though I've just landed a part in an epic Western adventure.

Pembrokeshire has always been rightly lauded for its beautiful coastline and its splendid islands, but just at this moment, I cannot imagine anywhere more majestic to be than in this unfolding tapestry of hills

Len Jones; Glynsaithmaen Farm

and fields before us. This is Mynydd Preseli in all its splendour. Talmynydd and Foel Cwmcerwyn stand on either side of us like a theatre's proscenium arch with the fields between a performance stage.

We start to climb and gallop at the same time – which is a new one for me. Carolyn shouts 'hold his mane' – I missed the rest of the sentence, but galloping on Blue along the lower slopes of the mountain is the most wonderfully exhilarating experience.

In the far corner of the field near Cerrig y Marchogion, a flock of sheep doesn't know yet that its quiet Saturday lunchtime is about to be disturbed by a shepherd on his horse, a pack of sheepdogs and a camera crew who will no doubt require a retake.

When we finally catch up with Len he is sitting on Rock at the top of the hill, surveying the land around him like an ancient general commanding a few loyal troops. I have watched sheepdogs being put through their paces many times, but what follows leaves me open-mouthed. With a few words his dogs seem to

Len Jones and Rock at work

become remote-controlled; at one moment they're sprinting at speeds that would seem impossible, then stopping abruptly; they look back at Len, then stare intently at the sheep. The dogs seem to be psyching the sheep to make the right move next. Working with camera crews, it's usual to expect them *not* to be impressed by whatever they're filming – they've usually seen it all before – but this orchestral performance of one man on his horse is masterly and humbling. When

I'm old, I'll look back on days like today and remember that this has been a special privilege.

Sheep rounded up, the dogs return to the side of Len's horse like scouts whose mission is proudly accomplished, and it's time for us to say goodbye. Len races them back to the farmyard and I wonder as I watch them disappear into the trees if I've been caught in some time-lapsed afternoon from another century and another world.

A horse knows when it's a good time to gallop, and for a change, Blue's got the wind behind him. On these open mountain pastures, the constrictions of riding on the roads are gone. It doesn't take much for me to initiate opening up the throttle for some wilder riding. And not for the first time Carolyn looks mildly alarmed at my beginner's over-confidence.

It's a short afternoon's ride from the farm to Bryn Morris, past two standing stones and the ordered trees at Glynaeron below Cnwc Rhudd's unkind gradient. The artist Elizabeth Haines's house is painted in a deep earthy, reddish-brown that stands out for miles against the green of the forests on the flanks of Cnwc Rhudd, and the flat fields on which it sits. The house and gallery are at the end of a long lane, and our clip-clopping brings her out to greet us. She makes tea and fetches a bucket of water for the horses.

I don't mind admitting a certain relief on dismounting. This is the longest I've ever been in a saddle, and as I reach my leg over Blue and drop to the flagstones, I know that Elizabeth must be aware that I'm moving uneasily. Now I know why John Wayne walked the way he did.

Elizabeth has converted the old cowshed into an artist's studio. At one end, there's a gallery of framed landscapes behind glass and on the table, there's a box of prints, hermetically sealed in cellophane.

Elizabeth was working until we arrived, and as I take a look at her past paintings, I catch sight of her reflection in a glass frame, back at her easel at the other end of the studio, paintbrush in hand, staring at the canvas she's brushing.

Elizabeth has been painting the Preseli landscape

Elizabeth Haines in her studio

Corrugated zinc in the real landscape and in paintings by Elizabeth Haines

for nearly forty years; her paintings capture the bleak, empty ancient beauty of the hills. Maybe it takes an artist to show the uniqueness of this beguiling place; her studies of blasted trees clinging to the shallow earth, stunted hedgerows sheltering frozen sheep, and achingly isolated farmsteads look like something from *Wuthering Heights*.

There is one of her paintings that makes me stop and stare; it is a canvas of a cold green mountain landscape that is the dominant feature of the painting, save for a tiny, red zinc-roofed barn in the centre of the work that is dwarfed by the natural world around it. Its depiction of a cold, harsh winter in these isolated hills makes me shiver. Her work encapsulates what living and working in these mountains has meant for generations of people.

I could happily stand and watch an artist work for hours. I have no artistic ability myself and the greatest of respect for those who have. But through the window, I see the horses are restless and snorting loudly at my timekeeping; they're ready for the next stage of their Preseli adventure, even if my backside could do with another half an hour's break and another cuppa.

The sun washing across the hills on the other side of the fields this afternoon would have been the perfect inspiration for Elizabeth. First it was watery and tentative, sheltering behind clouds and then roaring like fire, lighting up intense green, yellow and purple in the layers of moorland. In the first few hours of the early afternoon it has changed the landscape a thousand times. I can see why so many artists flock here; there is something really special about the light.

THE BLUESTONE CONTROVERSY

Aled Hughes

Who would have thought that prehistoric stones could generate such controversy? And spotted ones at that! But there's more than academic reputation at stake in the debate about the origin of the Stonehenge bluestones – there's passion! For that was surely the power behind the ill-fated attempt to re-enact a hypothetical 4,000-year-old journey from the Preseli hills to Wiltshire, 240 miles away. It had long been known that at least some of the so-called bluestones in the inner circle and horseshoe at Stonehenge originated from Pembrokeshire and that the two main types of bluestone (dolerite and spotted dolerite) are to be found together in a small area around Carn Menyn. This had led to speculation that people had transported the 'magical' stones all the way to Stonehenge for ritual reasons, or for some sophisticated astronomical project. Unfortunately the weighty stone selected for the re-enactment was only 17 miles into its millennium trip when disaster struck. It had been hard going from the very beginning even when the stone was being hauled along modern road surfaces, but the crunch came as, in the process of

being rowed across the Milford Haven waterway, it slipped unceremoniously into the sea.

To add insult to injury, it's debatable whether the adventure was worth undertaking in the first place, for many scientists believe that the bluestones were transported not by human but by glacier power. Pembrokeshire geology expert Brian John has long argued that the bluestones were carried from different locations across the Preseli Hills by glaciers and over fifteen years ago his argument found support from researchers at the Open University. On the other hand, others, who conveniently ignore the fact that the bluestones are a collection of different rock types, claimed to have found the exact location of the Preseli 'quarry', a source of made-to-measure pillars for the building of the ancient temple at Stonehenge.

There's no doubt that the idea of prehistoric man deliberately selecting and then transporting stones for hundreds of miles has a stronger hold on the popular imagination than the thought that they arrived by geological accident, however convincing the argument.

Tafarn Sinc, Rosebush: the watering-hole

Our destination next day is only a few miles down the narrow road between Mynachlog-ddu and Rosebush. David Jennings of Pant-mawr farm in Rosebush left very clear instructions on the phone a few days ago: 'Make sure you set out early enough because you'll need time to change and get all the gear on.'

When we arrive, David, his wife Cynthia and son Jason are taking a delivery from a milk tanker. Once the vehicle has done its rounds of the small farms around the hills, it empties its cargo, by way of a hose, into a vast, waist-high, stainless-steel tank.

It's probably a while since anyone arrived at Pant-mawr on horseback, but the hygiene instructions are the same for all visitors. As Carolyn leads the horses off to graze behind the scraggly farm buildings, I exchange my riding hat for a white hairnet and don an oversized clinical gown. Riding boots are left outside and I pad into the barn in disinfected white wellingtons.

Behind the plastic curtain, the ancient wall of slate and stone hides a scrubbed operation that is cleaner than an operating theatre. The air is thick with a slightly sweet, sickly scent of milk. I hope they won't notice that I smell a bit horsey. David motions me to scrub my hands.

David, Cynthia and Jason are all leaning over the vast tank and sieving off solids from the liquid which pours from the bottom of each of their leaking vessels. They don't stop to talk, but work quickly and at the same time explain how this unpromising warm wash will soon become delicious cheese.

David gives me a container the size of a small bucket and we all work together to gather the cheese, which is pretty back-breaking stuff, particularly when your other end is aching from a day in the saddle.

After a few minutes my nose itches, and I scratch it without thinking. David tells me to stop working immediately and repeat the whole disinfection process again. Their work is too highly prized to allow any risks of infection.

Chastised, nose scratched, hands cleaned again and it's back to the cheese-making.

'Everyone always does that the first time,' smiles Cynthia, frantically gathering the solids in her bowl.

The soft warm cheese is dropped from our small containers into larger moulds, which David carries over to drip onto racks on the other side of the barn. They don't ram the cheese into the moulds and in that way it won't become compacted.

'It means our cheeses are airy and sponge-like in texture, rather than hard,' David explains.

It takes the four of us the best part of an hour to process what feels like hundreds of gallons of liquid. I've never made cheese before, and there is something rather satisfying about producing something to eat, after riding past herds of cows who've so generously contributed.

My arms are aching, though, from bowling through so much liquid for an hour.

When our work is done, Cynthia and Jason begin the forensic cleaning of their equipment, while David shows me out of the barn to another outbuilding. Taking off your hairnet and white gown together can be a curiously bonding experience. I have to lean against the door to take off my protective clothing, the combined exercise of the horse and the cheesemaking having left few of my limbs in full supportive order.

In another outbuilding across the yard, the delightful aroma of yellowing and golden cheeses hits me before we swing open the door. Yesterday's cheeses are maturing on huge wooden racks. They look like perfect round cakes. It would be almost unkind to cut them.

David finds a small knife under a counter, and like a jeweller offering precious stones to a customer, he pushes one of his masterpieces towards me.

'This is Caws Cerwyn. All our cheeses are named after the hills. This has a light and fluffy taste. Try a bit?'

My God, it's like nectar, it's delicious. I wonder if it's bad form to ask for more at a cheese-tasting. I've missed lunch and feel absolutely ravenous. It's all this fresh air.

David seems heartened that he's not in the presence of one of those who watches his weight, and is clearly keen to offer more of his cheeses.

'Caws Preseli is a soft mould-ripened cheese, tangy and fruity with a rich taste.'

He's got the branding patter off to a tee for those crucial few moments you have to persuade potential customers at farmers' markets in Haverfordwest.

Blessed are the cheesemakers

Foel Cwmcerwyn, where winters are often harsh

This is even better than the last one. I help myself to another slice. I feel momentarily guilty that Carolyn is outside somewhere and probably peckish too, but it would be rude to leave David now, while he's in full flow.

The small wooden-handled knife cuts another wedge from a different cake of cheese.

'This one is a particular favourite, this is oak-smoked Cerwyn. You must taste this before you go. It matures for five or six months.'

Oh, go on then. It's delicious, like all the others, and I help myself to another small sliver.

And now I'm stuffed. The punishment of a glutton – a belly full of the most delicious handmade cheese.

David fastens the shop door (no one seems to lock their doors here) and we both look out at the late afternoon's shadows creeping over the moorland beneath the summit of Foel Cwmcerwyn and Foel Eryr.

The Preseli Hills are not the easiest place to make a living; the land and its location is challenging. Whilst artists and craftsmen thrive in this solitude, north Pembrokeshire is so far from the markets of cities it has been historically difficult to make businesses work here, other than in larger and larger farms or in tourism (so often dependent on the seasons and the weather).

The holiday homes, struggling post offices, few shops or garages and declining schools, tell their own story of an economy where the young often leave for opportunities elsewhere. So you can't help feeling delight that David and his family are building a viable business in the heart of the mountains that keeps local people in jobs. But it is clearly an uphill struggle and working in the Preseli Hills now is as hard as it's always been.

Having been given such a huge spread of free samples to taste, I clutch a whole Caws Preseli for the waiting crew and Caroline to eat.

My legs and back are aching from two day's riding, my arms are about to drop off from the unfamiliar exercise of cheese-making, and I have a very full stomach. Getting back on Blue for the final stretch may take a bit of doing.

We plod slowly across the Preseli bridleways, too tired to talk much – and anyway, Caroline is happily chewing her cheese. The farms and cottages hide in the bleak and empty valley sheltering in the hills from the Atlantic's worst blasts. Near Foel Eryr we are high enough to look down on yellow and green fields spread out like dark-edged handkerchiefs. A bird living close to the path, sensing homelessness, startles the horses for a moment. Shadows of grey clouds float over the hills delaying their deluge – until later, when they'll punish Carmarthenshire.

Off the hill now, we head into Cwm Gwaun. And at Dyffryn Arms there's some very welcome liquid refreshment, poured from a jug and it's frothy. Bessie Davies is a formidable landlady – this is a proper Pembrokeshire pub. There's no food served here, just beer.

As we climb further towards Carn Ingli, I know I should lean forward in the saddle to help Blue climb our last hill. I can feel both his energy and mine is failing with the day. Suddenly we're on a purple-flecked carpet of bright heather and young yellow gorse which is home to a thousand bees hovering above its bright colours. Its pungent aroma, strong now on the cooler air, takes me back to our visits here in short

Dyffryn Arms; Bessie Davies; Pont-faen

trousers, when our parents would wax lyrical at the heather and gorse in full bloom and my brothers and I would fancy ourselves as sheep rustlers or wild natives. Invariably, before making for home, Gran would tell us to leap out of the car once more and search for scraps of sheep's wool for her corns. It was years later that we rumbled this as a trick to exhaust three small children before the long drive back to Pembroke Dock.

In the far distance, beyond Dinas Head, the ferry leaves Fishguard's safety and, toy-like on a mill pond, points to Ireland's shores.

The horses know this path well and need no direction or encouragement. They are on the last lap of a well-trod route. This is nearly the end of their trail and mine – they too can see the sweep of Newport Bay on our horizon. In an hour we will ride across the beach and cool their tired feet in the cold tide before dark.

In the sun's sudden absence, the sky paints an impossible canvas of orange and red streaks that will silence those sailors returning on their boats. Tomorrow I will watch this huge sky become small in my mirrors and wonder how much more of my life I will spend leaving a place that I love so much.

Dyfed Elis-Gruffydd

Above: The intrepid Owen brothers; below: Dinas Head

High and dry, Parrog, Newport

ON THE WRITER'S
TRAIL

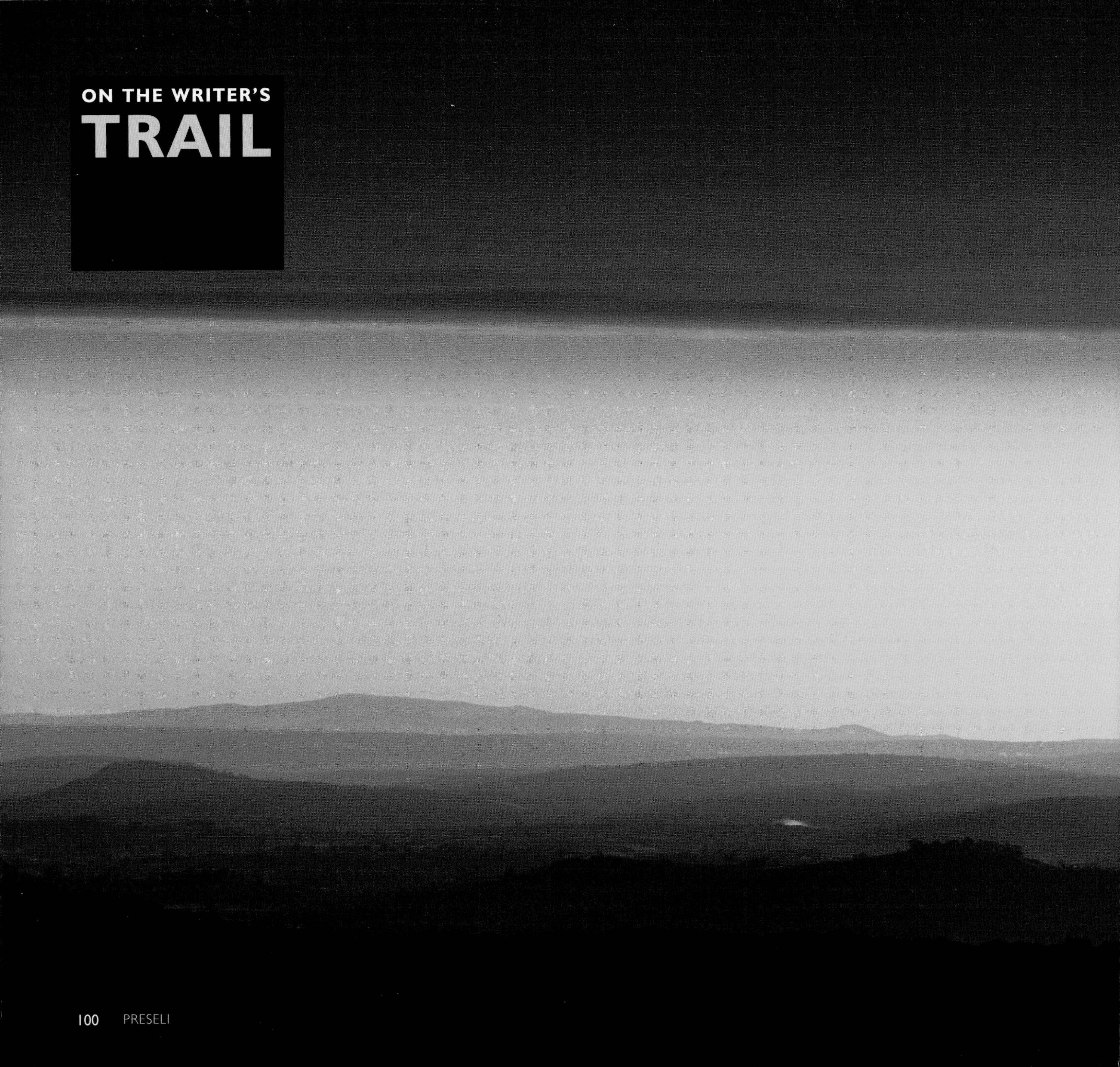

Glyndŵr's Parliament building is modest and understated, almost monastic in its simplicity. Its ancient slate, stone and timbers the only remaining witnesses to so much promise centuries before.

In Machynlleth, the high street is how high streets used to be. There's an ironmonger's, a butcher's and a baker's. The tall toy-town clock is bedecked by 'Save our Clock' posters. They've stretched bunting high across the streets to celebrate the Machynlleth Festival, and the coming days will see some of the country's top musicians fill The Tabernacle with delighted audiences.

Back on Maengwyn Street, a tractor and trailer full of sheep is double parked and causing gridlock Machynlleth-style. Intriguing little passages run off the main roads to the stables of the town's old coaching inns. Green cafés, art galleries, wholefood stores, a home-brew and pet shop, and a second-hand book store with a note in the window advising 'back after lunch', all tell you that this place has decided that chain stores, supermarkets and shopping malls are not for them.

Machynlleth is a civic version of a giant two fingers to convention. It's a retreat from the madness of the rest of the world, the home of original thinkers, radicals and idealists.

A few miles up the road, hiding in an old slate quarry, you'll find the Centre for Alternative Technology.

Standing above the steep, hydro-powered cliff railway, Christine McLennan clutches a family album from the time when she and her husband Roger first came to Machynlleth twenty-five years ago. At the time, these 'weirdo drop outs' were regarded with a great deal

Machynlleth

of either suspicion or amusement. The early founders of CAT were described in the world outside as the 'shit and wind' brigade. People couldn't understand why normal folk would give up on the 'necessities' of mains electricity, water and material wealth.

But those early critics were probably of their time and it was the founders of CAT, such as Christine and Roger, who were ahead of the game. What started as an alternative way of life for a few far-sighted believers has now become mainstream thinking. When the leader of the Conservative Party puts a wind turbine on his roof, you know the landscape has changed forever.

It's high summer and this morning's early rain clouds have been burnt off by a warming sun. The centre is filling with dozens of families with children.

Just watching the people around me this morning, I'm taken by how committed the children are to protecting the environment, perhaps more so than their parents.

Jeremy Moore

Centre for Alternative Technology

It was different in our house when we were kids; the catalyst for thinking about the environment was my father, who would switch off lights in unoccupied rooms, to a derisive chorus of siren noises made by my brothers and me.

My father grew up in a house in Pembrokeshire during the Depression. The generation clash between us couldn't have been more profound. His early life in a poor community informed his behaviour for the rest of his days. In his legal practice, to the bemusement of his staff, he would send letters in recycled envelopes, partly no doubt to save money, but chiefly because he couldn't bear waste.

He wore his father's tweed jackets and when he needed a car he bought a Mini. His carbon footprint on the earth was small (except for the contribution to global warming made by smoking his pipe).

At the dining table, if you left food, he would shovel it onto his plate rather than throw it away. He could never understand why anyone would spend money on conspicuous materialism like big houses, large cars, lavish holidays or clothes. It was unnecessary and unsustainable.

My grandparents were the same. The idea that you would throw anything away was inconceivable. Inside their cottage there was a stone-floored pantry where a bucket of cold water kept bottles of milk cold; pheasants and hams hung from the rafters; there was no fridge or freezer, no washing machine or tumble dryer, and my grandfather stood still in front of a light switch every time he turned it on, in proud celebration of this small miracle. They had one car that lasted them for forty years, and when it broke they mended it.

I tell you this not in any desire to return to some smock-wearing medieval existence. My parents and grandparents grew up in a rural Wales without electricity, mains gas or telephone but I am a child of the take-away generation. We see something we like: we must have it now, even if we don't really need it or we can't afford it. My generation, and I include myself in this, live in houses that burn energy even when empty. I'll bet some of the visitors to CAT today have left electrical appliances on standby and the hot water will come on whether there is anyone home to use it or not. If they are anything like an average household, they will throw away 40% of the food they buy. None of this is criticism, but as I sit here drinking my cuppa looking at the wind turbines, the solar panels and the houses of the future, I feel more than a little guilty for my part and my generation's pursuit of material wealth that is costing the earth.

The car park is full with the usual quota of four-wheel drive cars and gas guzzlers, but at least the drivers have come to listen to the arguments. We delay leaving until Christine has said goodbye, just in case she sees how many vehicles we arrived in to film our documentary.

Somewhere on the road to the twenty-first century we thought that the pursuit of a life championing excess rather than moderation was sustainable, and now we know it's not. With their vegetable patches, compost toilets and wind turbines, they had hit on that truth in Machynlleth long before the rest of us.

A generation reared in a natural playground

OWAIN GLYNDŴR

In proclaiming himself Prince of Wales and leading a rebellion against the English king, Henry IV, Owain Glyndŵr ensured a place for all time in the hearts and minds of Welsh people. Not just a brave warrior, Glyndŵr was a man of culture and an astute politician with far-sighted ambitions for his country such as the establishment of universities in both north and south Wales and the securing of independence from English institutions. Owain Glyndŵr inherited royal blood from both his parents and his campaign against English oppression began when a neighbouring lord laid claim to his land in the Welsh borders.

Spectacular military successes provoked crushing resistance from the English crown, with savage retaliation against some of Glyndŵr's supporters. His influence and power nevertheless increased until 'like a second Assyrian' he overthrew the castles of Usk, Caerleon and Newport. Manoeuvres and counter-manoeuvres continued the length and breadth of Wales until in 1404 Owain held a parliament at Machynlleth. Although the existing Parliament House dates from after Glyndŵr's time, it is possible that it was constructed from materials taken from the site of the original parliament. It is likely that he chose Machynlleth because of its central location and because it was an area where he exercised political control. It is said that it was here that Glyndŵr was crowned Prince of Wales.

Despite significant military success, Owain Glyndŵr eventually lost ground and was defeated, his wife and daughters being imprisoned in the Tower of London. The Welsh revolt ultimately failed because Wales could not maintain a sustained rebellion in the face of punitive English sanctions. Although he might have been expected to meet a bloody fate, Glyndŵr's actual destiny remains mysterious. He just seems to have disappeared. Shakespeare's hint at magical powers for this most enigmatic of national heroes may well be justified.

Wind farm at Carno

Outside Carno, a few miles down the road, you'll find one of the modern wonders of Wales. Not an ancient castle or a cathedral, but a huge wind farm. Whether you like wind farms or not, this construction has changed the landscape on a spectacular scale. Trannon Moor has been a working landscape for centuries; you'll find standing stones here, a Bronze Age cairn, and evidence of peat-cutting. The skies are the familiar territory of red kite, hen harrier, buzzard, red grouse, curlew and golden plover – all of which make unlikely bedfellows with the giant sweeping white blades.

When it was built ten years ago, this was the most powerful wind farm in Europe, serving the energy needs of thirteen thousand homes. This, we are told, is the future, or at least part of the future. There are fifty-six turbines around me, each one over thirty metres high, and the diameter of the rotas is forty-four metres. I feel as though I have walked onto the set of a science-fiction film.

My car is dwarfed by the turbine nearest the road. As far as the eye can see in every direction, there are whirring blades. Stand close enough and you can hear the clunking noise emanating from their innards. A rhythmic and almost mesmeric whoosh, whoosh, whoosh follows you around as you wander beneath blades that are too high to hit your head, but low enough to thrill. Each turbine takes up a tiny fragment of land but the visual impact is immense.

Each turbine has a little ladder up the side of it, as though Windy Miller might pop out at any moment and make a brew. Standing on the little platform halfway up the white tower, I'm at first overawed by the sheer scale of the project, but the more I look at the extent of the turbines covering the hills, the less comfortable I feel. When I ask the film crew and Martyn, the photographer, what they think of this unusal tourist attraction and its impact on Wales, they are evenly divided in their opinions – just like the great general public.

I love this countryside, its rolling mountains and its shady valleys, and I don't want to see all of upland Wales covered in wind farms like this. I don't really want wind farms, or nuclear or gas-fired power stations, or oil refineries. But in the real world, our need for power is increasing exponentially and wind farms are perhaps an inevitable part of the solution. For all the controversy, when they are spinning, they do make for a spectacular sight. I grew up in the shadow of Pembroke's oil-fired power station which belched its bad breath into the sky. At least this place won't store up so many unanswered health questions like oil, or gas, or leave nuclear waste for another generation. All the same, the inspiration, the calmness and wilderness of the Welsh countryside is also an important part of everyone's inheritance. There are no easy answers on this journey, only more questions.

Back to the car – it's a small efficient diesel – is that ok? It's an uncomfortable thought that man has done more damage to the planet in the last two hundred

*Montgomeryshire
countryside; the
Humphreys children*

years than the last two thousand. Just think of the forests sawn down and the seas that have been drained.

You'd think our carnage of the Earth would stop when we die, but no. Between Newtown and Montgomery, near Dolforwyn Castle, you'll find another intriguing place that's not on the sightseer's map. Green Lane Burial Site caters for those who don't want to pollute the earth when they die. So far it's one of the few green burial sites in Wales.

Ifor Humphreys, his wife Eira and their children are playing in the fields with the dog when I arrive. They once were preoccupied with lamb and beef production but the trials of making a living from farming forced them to diversify and consider what else they could do with their land. Their conclusion was that they could make a living out of dying.

The warm grass of the meadow in which we sit is the final resting place of twenty-one people who have been buried without headstones, marble crosses or family vaults. Instead a small pebble with a number marks their graves.

When you think about it, nothing could be more arrogant than to spend a lifetime polluting the planet and then continue to do so after death. Think of the madness of the rituals and traditions surrounding bereavement. A perfectly good tree is chopped down to make a coffin. That in turn is swathed in everlasting brass handles and other decorations. If you are cremated, the smoke (not to mention the mercury from your fillings) poisons the air. If you're buried, the efforts to make you and your coffin look presentable will take years to break down. So much for ashes to ashes and dust to dust.

Eira disappears inside the house to make one of those farmhouse teas to die for, while Ifor walks around the acre on the hill dedicated to burials. It's a lovely spot. When you think of all the municipal graveyards that lie overgrown and untended you wonder why more people wouldn't want somewhere like this as their final resting place.

High on this green hill I can see for miles each way down the valley where the River Severn is still narrow enough to wade across.

'Come and look at the graves,' says Ifor in one of the more unusual invitations of my short career.

The soft yellowing turf cooked gently by the hot summer, starved of rain for so many weeks, suddenly changes texture. On closer examination, I can see it's shaped into uneven squares that have been returned to the ground.

On a tree trunk nearby the words 'Lewis Chadwick aged 19' have been carved gently into the soft bark.

A few feet away, a large pebble is the only mark that denotes 29-year-old Stephen Harvey.

'So many of us live rootless lives,' says Ifor. 'It's nonsensical to be buried in a churchyard with which you had no connection in life, and in death is too remote for your family to attend to. The conventions of the church are no longer a part of many people's lives so those buried here decide their death should be no different.'

A rabbit sits on the bank and watches us for a moment before disappearing into the brambles. For the people buried here, their deaths will be as their lives were: walked lightly upon the earth.

I've always thought that you should judge a man by his shed. Ifor's sheds contain a variety of biodegradable coffins: one made from bamboo, another of willow and cardboard. It's interesting watching the reaction of the crew while we wander around and talk about something that will be a certainty for us all; even among youngish people of my age for whom there are so few subjects that are off-limits, death really is still the last taboo.

Iolo Williams

Green Lane burial field

I have sailed around the coastline of Wales by lifeboat, jogged over the now abandoned branch railway lines of mid-Wales and marched around the country in the formidable footsteps of George Borrow.

This exercise became an important part of my life. It was my annual escape from the great Slab World that is slowly closing in on us all. Escape used to be a dirty word in my youth, but as the shape of the future becomes clearer, escapism becomes

respectable. Very few people indeed can master the techniques required for living the happy life in our fully mechanised, air-conditioned, noise-pervaded, mind-controlled society. I know that I am not among these happy few.

Wynford Vaughan-Thomas (1908-1987),
from *Madly in All Directions*

Restoration at Tŷ Mawr

It's time to continue our journey. The road to Llangors Lake is a wonderful treat on a warm summer's afternoon. The trees and hedges are in full leaf and the fields hazy in the heat. From Newtown the old coach road to Brecon is heavy with ambling caravans enjoying the hills and valleys sweeping around the river Ithon. An increasingly long line of irate followers snakes behind in their cars, waiting for their chance to dash for freedom.

Nigel Gervis and his wife Joyce are waiting for us on the lawn of their rambling farmhouse on the banks of Llangors Lake. When I was in school we used to come here to learn to sail. I can remember looking over the lake and seeing this beautiful old house and wondering who lived here. It wasn't Nigel and Joyce then; they've only been here for thirteen years.

They are making a name for themselves in the alternative building world. In this ancient house, constructed in haphazard fashion over many centuries, they are championing environmentally-friendly construction. Like most people, I am so used to hearing about car and air travel as the familiar targets of environmental criticism that the building industry's contribution to poisoning the planet is a new one on me.

Joyce and Nigel run a company called Tŷ Mawr Lime. They launched it at the same time as they bought this run-down house – as a result of trying to source materials to renovate it. Over a decade later they are Wales's largest specialist producers of lime mortars, plasters, daubs and lime washes and they sell over two hundred ecological building products. Their house is listed and inevitably governed by a myriad of regulations relating to restoration materials. Researching what is allowed, and tracking down tradesmen with relevant skills, has given birth to a successful business. But it's also introduced them to understanding how many of our houses contribute to the story of environmental damage.

You wouldn't think of the building industry as one of the major ecological villains – easier perhaps to visualise traffic fumes and plastic shopping bags as the destructive by-products of modern living. Excavating land for foundations, extracting sand for cement, brewing chemicals to make paint and timber treatments, and dumping of construction waste are some of the biggest contenders for the 'dirty man of Europe' awards.

The two children stay on the lawn and play with Joyce while Nigel gives us the guided tour around the house and gardens. Nigel explains that their biggest development has been to recycle waste glass, now used instead of sand in construction work. Switzerland recycles 95% of its glass, but for Britain it's 25%.

Like a proud estate agent, he points out the labour of love that it has taken to turn around the fortunes of this once-ruined home. Joyce shouts from the garden, 'Don't forget to tell them about our trialling of hemp products to replace chemically-produced insulation.' He forgets anyway.

The cynics will say it's all very well to pursue this agenda for a piecemeal single-building renovation but it's not a runner for a mass construction project like a housing estate. However, after listening to Joyce's list of nasty chemicals that go to make up the average house and hearing about the damaging impact of the

Above: Llangors Lake, below: Tŷ Mawr

CENTRE FOR ALTERNATIVE TECHNOLOGY

The Centre for Alternative Technology has been a vital source of inspiration for thinking about the environment and its challenges for more than thirty years. Set up in 1973 as an eco-friendly community and a testing-ground for new technology, CAT has been educating visitors from its earliest days, and opened its first visitor centre in 1975. Regarded initially as a rather quaint or eccentric distraction from the 'real' world, CAT's pioneering innovations and practical ideas are now receiving serious attention from people keen to 'do their bit' for a greener future. Such is the anxiety about our impact on the planet.

For the environmentally-responsible, a visit to CAT could lead to a whole new way of life, whether this means learning how to build a house with the very latest energy-saving ideas, or learning how to maintain a garden kind to birds and wildlife. At CAT, ideas for composting extend well beyond conventional household waste, with a range of toilet alternatives sure to impress even the most lavatorially minded. Recycling is the order of the day, with fun ideas for children as well as adults. Visitors may find themselves inspired to install their own wind-turbines or solar panels when they get home, though harnessing wave power may be beyond the capacity of the suburban householder! The Centre offers a comprehensive vision for an alternative lifestyle. Whether driven by curiosity or conscience, you can't fail to be impressed by the range of inspirational projects.

standard construction process, my earlier preoccupation with four by fours and long-haul flights has acquired a new focus. As with the Centre for Alternative Technology, the campaign here for more environmentally-friendly building techniques will take years to catch on, but one day their use will be taken for granted.

The grounds of this old house would be a good place to linger, watching the little dinghies fly across Llangors Lake, but our plan is to travel to the other side of the Brecon Beacons before the late afternoon shadows become too long for filming.

At the side of Pen-y-fan, near Libanus, Theresa Toomey and Ian Henderson are working in their vegetable field. They look something like Tom and Barbara from *The Good Life*, but this is no TV sitcom.

Surrounded by a pack of suspicious dogs who have taken an instant dislike to our tardy timekeeping, I am immediately enlisted to pick carrots – which don't look anything like the rather insipid specimens in my local supermarket.

The six dogs seem to travel in convoy behind us with two cats and a number of deranged chickens. Two Jersey cows and six horses in the field opposite pointedly ignore us at all times.

Despite the advice of nearby farmers against growing crops this high up a mountain, Ian and Theresa have proved the doubters wrong. Theresa is the driving force behind Beacons Veggie Boxes, who deliver locally-grown produce to the local community. She is vociferously critical of the unquestioning transportation of food across the country, of chemically-propagated farming and our dislocation from the food we eat.

Picking and packing vegetables

Down on the farm

'Remember,' she barks, shaking the earth from a huge bunch of orange carrots, 'Wales has one of the highest rates of obesity in Europe, more heart disease than the average western country and it all starts with the food we eat.'

Theresa and Ian have tapped into what so many people already know – the majority of us are eating processed rubbish and it's making us fat. Their desire to promote a connection back to the farm has seen families turn up here for the simple excitement of pulling crops from the ground. Who'd have thought that children would consider spending the day picking potatoes, carrots, turnips, strawberries an exciting and thrilling summer-holiday activity?

It would be foolish to pretend that a couple of well-meaning and far-sighted food campaigners like Theresa and Ian will switch society's love affair with its supermarkets, but the success of their farm home-deliveries is mirrored in other communities the length and breadth of the country. Theresa and Ian might be voices on the fringe but as I walk past the cardboard boxes being packed in the barn, I know that their belief in what they are doing is well-founded. We have an odd relationship with food. We know eating the wrong stuff makes us ill and overweight, and yet we continue to wilfully make the wrong choices – knowingly shortening our lives.

It takes an hour to travel from Brecon to Penarth. This is the end of our journey – a beach looking over the Bristol Channel at sunset. I'm here to meet the artist Terry Setch. He's on the far shore looking down on the beach, clutching a handful of rubbish.

Setch uses the detritus he finds on this small stretch

of shore – plastic packaging, tins, cling film and glass, to make large paintings. They are not pretty works and they are not comfortable to look at either, but he pricks the conscience, which makes it sobering and worthwhile.

'Since the 1980s, I've been finding so much more plastic, much less glass; we're poisoning the sea,' Terry laments, stooping down to pick up another piece of flotsam.

We get some odd looks from the other walkers out for an evening stroll.

Later in his studio, we look at some of his recent canvasses – massive works that are bigger than him. I can't remember the last time I looked at any art that made me shudder. But having to confront the yards of water-borne rubbish, the everlasting memorials to the world of packaging that Terry captures in his work, he's made me think about my own shopping habits.

It's a wrap and goodbyes to the crew on the pavement before we set off in different directions. This has been an odd journey; I had expected our travels through the temples of sustainable living in Wales to deliver some culprits after our investigations. I know you shouldn't ever begin any journalistic enterprise with preconceptions, but I had expected to deliver a confident final piece to camera to finish off the film. I had expected to point a finger at the world's oil industry, the power companies, the nuclear lobby, the supermarkets or the shipping industry and criticise them for their unsustainable ways. But the most uncomfortable conclusion I come to is that, while all of them have a huge responsibility to secure the planet's future, there is another huge responsibility to be apportioned too: my own. My choices, my footprint on the earth, my house, my shopping, my car, my office, my food, my packaging, my life. It's all too easy for an individual to shift blame onto others. I don't know if journeys change you, but this more than most has made me think about the way I live my life.

Terry Setch with art made from shoreline debris at Penarth

ON THE WRITER'S
TRAIL

Jeremy Moore

THE MORNING-WATCH

O joys! Infinite sweetness! with what flowers
And shoots of glory, my soul breaks and buds!
        All the long hours
        Of night and rest,
      Through the still shrouds
      Of sleep, and clouds,
   This dew fell on my breast;
      O how it bloods,
And spirits all my earth! hark! in what rings,
And hymning circulations the quick world
       Awakes, and sings!
       The rising winds,
      And falling springs,
      Birds, beasts, all things
    Adore Him in their kinds.
       Thus all is hurl'd
In sacred hymns and order; the great chime
And symphony of Nature. Prayer is
       The world in tune,
       A spirit-voice,
      And vocal joys,
Whose echo is heaven's bliss.

Henry Vaughan (1621-1695)

GOWER

SEASIDE CAMPING

Over fifty years ago, Gower was declared Britain's first Area of Outstanding Natural Beauty. It's no wonder that such a dramatic

Three Cliffs Bay

Aled Hughes

and unspoilt peninsula as Gower was chosen. Dylan Thomas
played his part in making it famous as well, of course – this was
the seaside of his boyhood, a place to camp and woo the girls.

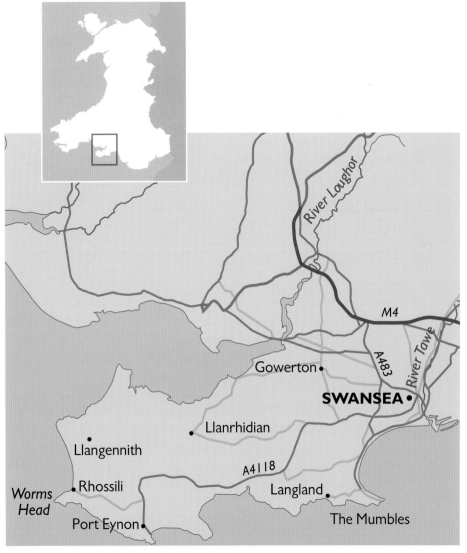

ON THE FAR SIDE OF THE WATER FROM Mumbles, the dirty black and red freighter lying low in the water looks almost out of place now; that's how much Swansea has changed. The vessel slinks slowly out to sea as though turning its back on the sprouting yuppie flats climbing above the roofs of the marina.

The Mumbles side of the bay has always been slightly removed from the historic heavy industry of its neighbouring port. Its streak of shops, small hotels, and cafés clings to the bottom of the rocks. This is where people come to escape work; this is Swansea's playground.

I've always wondered about the name 'Mumbles'. The languages they tried to teach me at school are rusty but one explanation for the name is that it derives from Latin 'mammae', Danish 'marmles' or French 'mamelles', all of which mean – and there is no delicate way of telling you this – 'breasts', a reference to the rocky inlets at the western edge of the bay. Just imagine being selected as a member of the new village-naming committee (this is Wales – so there would have had to have been a committee) and, after days of deliberation over a shortlist of names, coming up with that Eureka moment – 'I know, we'll call this place Breasts.'

I'm spending the weekend exploring Gower. I'm someone who always drives past this part of the world on the way to or from somewhere else. So for once, I'm going to stay a while and get to know it better. I need some appropriate transport for this adventure and after careful consideration what better way to explore this beach bum's Mecca than a 1966 VW camper van? Unfortunately I don't own one but I know a man who does and he's on his way.

Why do vintage Volkswagens make such an extraordinary noise? Perhaps the engineers knew the brakes and steering were awful and deliberately made the vehicle noisy so at least the unwary would know it was coming.

Adam Shore is a Volkswagen fanatic. He is clearly in two minds about letting a rather dodgy-looking camera crew and me borrow his pride and joy for the weekend. These vehicles are like gold dust: Adam's VW is forty years old and imported from California.

'Like any forty-year-old it can be temperamental!' he smiles, shaking hands. He clearly loves his camper van. The interior smells of that whiff of elderly carpet and damp cardboard that has generously come free with every car I have ever owned. It's a heady combination of leatherette and leaking metal, though the passing of the years has blurred the distinction between the two materials.

The guided tour over, it's time for a test drive. Adam climbs into the passenger seat and winces as I engage the wrong gear again and again. The gears are close together, and don't have synchromesh to ease their change.

At my feet, I can see daylight, and realise why the camper doesn't sound any quieter inside than out: it's because of the holes in the pedal board.

The engine shrieks as I drive round the car park above Bracelet Bay. I'm just getting into the swing of it when Rob the television director decides what is needed is an arty opening sequence which involves me driving right over a small camera.

I'm never comfortable about doing things like this because they have a habit of going wrong, particularly if I'm involved. Twice we drive over the camera very

Above: One careful owner, Adam Shore; below: Mumbles lighthouse from Bracelet Bay

Oystermouth Castle; the pier;
overlooking Port Talbot

gently; and the little Japanese gizmo faithfully records the departure of the VW. And then a third take is called for 'just to have another one in the can'. The small hand-held camera has been placed on the tarmac, switched on and running, so that the VW's axles will pass over it with generous clearance.

At the sound of smashed electronic equipment, the television crew and Adam simultaneously cover their eyes, but only Adam is close enough for me to hear him gasp. He is about to hand over his beloved motor to a bunch of people who have just driven over a television camera.

The VW is not a straightforward drive. The narrow roads around Mumbles aren't the easiest even when you know where you are going and I'm balancing a map between my legs. The brakes need three days' written notice to stop and I'm not getting the hang of this gearbox. There won't be much staring out at the scenery this weekend; the VW requires you to mind-read every other road user – because by the time they've decided what they're going to do, it'll be too late for me. What I need now is a parking place – and one large enough for a bus.

Mumbles Lighthouse is taking a rest on this clear blue day. Far below its locked door, three children are on the beach exploring the rock pools. The early shifts of surfers are already in their black and purple skins but they'll be disappointed today – the water is as flat as a pancake.

In Verdi's it's always time for something to eat, and pink and white ice cream is already flying out of the door although it's still only breakfast time.

They're repairing Mumbles Pier this week. The

rotten skeleton of ancient gappy timbers is being pulled up and replaced with pale new wood. Thirty years of contempt for a faded old friend are being wire-brushed and painted over. A small army of pushchairs and cautious toddlers walks over the water, watching the waves through the cracks between the boards underfoot.

The anglers at the end of the pier stand on their own private shelf, staring at the city changing almost before their eyes across the bay. Each man has a large plastic box standing guard either side of him: one full of all the tackle for a long day's fishing, the other doubling up to carry food and drink or to sit on. No one's caught anything yet.

Alongside the pavement in Mumbles are the scruffy works in progress of chained-up local boats: some vessels for day fishing, others for dinghy racing; they are all a world away from the shiny plastic yachts sitting in the city's marina. 'The Antelope' looks wounded holding its broken keel and won't run again this summer.

Across the tarmac is a jumbled string of houses and shops, some delightful and others derelict, awaiting the kindly patronage of a developer.

Oystermouth Bowling Club is playing at home and is in the lead. The green has been washed, pressed and cut like soft felt; only the seagulls, spying to swoop on slowly-eaten chips, break the concentration of the silent white-coated teams.

The railings above the shore are propping up dozens like me looking out over the water. I can see Port Talbot's diminutive steel works from here; its Lilliput-like chimneys puff white wisps into the blue.

Sampling Verdi's ice-cream; the bowling green; on the promenade

ON THE WRITER'S TRAIL

Thursday, 18 April, 1872

. . . A tramway runs along the road side from Swansea to the Mumbles, upon which ply railway carriages drawn by horses.

Oystermouth Castle stands nobly upon a hill overlooking the town and bay. The lurid copper smoke hung in a dense cloud over Swansea, and the great fleet of oyster boats under the cliff was heaving in the greenest sea I ever saw. We had luncheon upon the cliffs overlooking the white lighthouse tower upon the most seaward of the Mumbles . . . A steam tug shot out of Swansea Harbour to meet a heavily laden schooner under full press of canvas in the bay and towed her into port, and the great fleet of oyster boats which had been out dredging was coming in round the lighthouse point with every shade of white and amber sails gay in the afternoon sun as they ran each into her moorings under the shelter of the great harbour cliff. As we went along the narrow cliff path amongst the gorse towards Langland and Caswell Bay, a flock of strange and beautiful black and white birds flew along the rock faces below us towards the lighthouse.

from the diary of Francis Kilvert (1840-1879)

Aled Hughes

GOWER DELICACIES

The name *Oystermouth* – for many years used interchangeably with the more-familiar *Mumbles* – gives us a big clue to one of Gower's former industries. The Mumbles oyster beds or perches were once an important part of the local economy, with evidence of a strong trade from medieval times onwards. They are now enjoying something of a revival after more than a century of serious decline. Today associated with the luxury end of the food market because of their scarcity and, perhaps, their reputation as an aphrodisiac, oysters were once enjoyed by ordinary Gower people as part of their staple diet.

In the seventeenth century, women were the key players, conducting the oyster-dredging operation from small rowing boats, and making an important contribution to the family income, as did that most iconic of Gower figures: the Penclawdd cockle-picker. The cockle-women would spend hours labouring on the mudflats of the Burry Inlet, donkeys laden with baskets carrying home the precious harvest. Today jeeps and tractors have taken the place of donkeys, but the art of cockle-gathering is essentially the same. Short-handled rakes are used to extricate the shellfish from the sand and sieves or riddles allow all but the biggest and most mature specimens to fall back through. These days a rigorous washing, cooking and packaging process ensures that only the finest cockles reach the buying public.

Another Gower delicacy – laver bread – is still processed at Penclawdd and its neighbouring villages. The washing and cooking to which the seaweed is subjected results in a dark glutinous product a bit like fishy spinach. An acquired taste, perhaps, laver bread is rightly prized for its mineral and vitamin content, with Welsh chefs inventive in their creation of new and delicious ways to serve this traditional Gower fare.

Oystermouth Castle; Oysters; Laver bread sauce with cockles; Welsh cheese and laver bread souffles

Further along the coast Porthcawl's distant pier will only be visible through the bolted telescope and I haven't got twenty pence to put in the slot.

The pavements are filled with tourists trying the ice-cream parlours, and local shoppers laden with groceries.

The crowds are out for the annual Mumbles Raft Race, which gets underway soon. The mad and the foolhardy begin to take to the water, racing in all manner of barely-floating home-made rafts, all to raise money for the Lifeboat. One entrant reversing a three-wheeler Reliant Robin down the slipway and into the water keeps us all entranced, particularly when, like some James Bond gadget, it not only doesn't sink, but begins to overtake other competitors. I'm going to leave before the end of the race before everybody else tries to.

It's a short winding drive to Langland Bay, and it's taking me a while to judge the width of the camper, so each oncoming car has me stamping on the brakes.

Langland is sheltered between two comforting arms; its safe flat gentle beach is watched over by scores of green and white wooden beach huts, each one with a pitched roof, all loftily leering at the reddening swimmers screaming in the cold waves.

It takes me several attempts to park the Volkswagen in the almost full car park; my wrestling with the steering wheel and then a second stall of the engine attracts the sympathy of the car park attendant who guides me into my final resting place.

As we walk past them, it's difficult not to sneak a curious look into each beach hut. We move on quickly when we realise we've gawped at two women

Plucky oarsmen

undressing in that most British of ceremonies: get-your-kit-off-at-the-beach-under-a-towel.

The huts are like little Tardises, home to folding chairs, a small table (also folding), picnic crockery, novels and newspapers, towels and drinks. Some have a little primus gas stove for ambitious lunches; others have heaving plastic bags on the floor stuffed with packets of crisps, sandwiches and pies bought from the garage up the road. What they all have is a view to die for. For two-hundred-and-fifty quid a year, you get a ringside seat at quite simply one of the most splendid sights in Britain: a lapping blue sea gently washing the sand and the endless fascination of a country at play. I've always thought it was rather peculiarly eccentric and British to go to the beach only to sit in a garden shed, but now the idea is fast growing on me.

Mr and Mrs Kemberry are at number 46 this year. They have rented a hut every year for fifty years. Mrs Kemberry has made lunch, and a generous spread of *bara brith*, Welsh cakes, a sponge and sandwiches is

The Kemberry beach hut

sitting enticingly on a tray out of the sun. A flask of tea stands next to cups and saucers on the table.

Mr Kemberry welcomes us at the door of his castle and offers folding chairs facing the sun. I can feel it burning my face within moments.

'The huts were built in Victorian times and are pretty run-down these days. Swansea Council lets them out for six months a year. Hundreds of local people apply to have their names put in a lottery and the lucky winners are drawn out of a hat. Oh and there's no running water or gas or electricity,' he smiles. The retired bank manager sits back down in his chair facing, as he has always done, right out to sea. He knows this is not just a good deal but the bargain of a lifetime.

Mrs Kemberry pours tea then milk from a jug, and cuts the cake. She produces a small pile of curling black-and-white photographs of the family playing here over the last four decades. Small snaps show cricket matches between the hut families, and old Polaroids capture picnics on the beach.

'There was quite a community here at one time, but we don't know all the people here now in the way that we used to,' she says, passing a slice of cream sponge.

Mr Kemberry reaches for his binoculars to look at a dinghy belting across the bay some distance from the shore. He was once a keen boatman but those days are long over.

I'm supposed to be interviewing Langland's longest-serving beach-hut dwellers but the cake is delicious, and Mrs K goes inside the hut for another slice for me, just as the crew say they are ready to begin filming.

She returns outside but sits just a little behind her husband, out of his eye line. They have spent so much of their lives together that they finish each other's answers and remember the other's forgotten moments.

Their newspapers are folded on the floor between us. The UK's airports are in chaos because of a terrorist plot. CANCELLED FLIGHTS, DAY LONG CHECK INS and NO HAND BAGGAGE scream the headlines.

The sun is blazing down on my neck. We pause to watch the teeming crowds on the beach below. I'm trying to think where else you ever see all the generations together in one place. Elderly sun worshippers lie on their sun loungers in the peace and quiet near the rocks. Elsewhere self-conscious teenagers are performing for each other, out for the day without their parents. Further along the shore, a little unsteady on their feet, preoccupied, wide-eyed, small children explore further than they are usually allowed before being shouted for.

There are three cricket games in progress, including one with a disbelieving batsman who won't leave his wicket and acknowledge he is out. On the wet sand a mixed volleyball match is in progress; a few yards above high-water mark, two wincing fathers are being buried alive by small and careless diggers and, oblivious to all the sporting action, fanatical engineers are busy digging gravity-defying ditches to channel the sea back up the sand.

The beach is in the blood if you live in Swansea. Today the kids playing here won't miss their computers, MP3 players, or watching the telly in their bedrooms. They are enjoying what their parents and grandparents have always known: an adventure that is both priceless and yet free.

The VW takes a few attempts to start and then finally the old girl splutters into life. After the ribbons of bungalows and villas overlooking the thronging bays and its thousands of visitors squeezed onto the narrow sand, the heart of Gower, that gentle land of hills and moors that runs through its middle, feels huge and empty. You have certain preconceptions when you explore a place for the first time and mine featured beach life and breathtaking cliff scenery. I had thought of Gower as having a spectacular coastline but little else. But just a few miles driving inland away from the sea, the miles of open countryside, and tucked-away cottages are the other side of a hidden and less-travelled Gower. These huge expanses of fields that run through the middle of the land are the heart of the place. It's only minutes from Swansea and all of the noise and bustle of a city, but this quiet retreat is another world away.

Above: Sun worshippers at Langland; below: inland Gower

Karl Jenkins;

A long way off the main road down a quiet rocky lane, composer Karl Jenkins is sitting in his old mill house at the keyboard when the music of an elderly air-cooled engine reaches his window. Wandering into the daylight all in black, he looks as a composer should: unworldly and distracted. His generous long moustache offers few clues to his mood until a giggle deep within declares his amusement. It is coffee time and while Richard and Annie set up their lights and cameras, Karl shows me around his house and garden. The rooms are full of mementos of a life in performance: a library of Grove's Music Dictionaries, and photographs of the composer at the podium conducting orchestras. Tucked out of the way is an antique chapel pedal-operated organ made homeless by the advent of electricity, and in his cramped book-lined study, is a keyboard wired to a computer. Knowing nothing about composing, I had thought that a composer sat at the ivories and swivelled around pen in hand scribbling notes on an empty manuscript, but Karl's flourish on the keys has the computer whirr into life and his every note is transcribed onto the screen ready to be emailed to studios or musicians.

Karl grew up not far from here, in Penclawdd, and after thirty years spent largely in London, he has come home. The radio station was playing his *Requiem* on my way here; it's rather odd five minutes later to be poured a large coffee by the great man himself.

'My father was the music teacher, organist and choirmaster of the village chapel. I think that being exposed to that tribal hymn singing was obviously hugely influential,' he says, passing me a steaming mug.

I assumed Karl had moved back here because the peace and quiet of Gower was more conducive for artists and musicians than the distractions of London, but he is too disciplined for that.

'I guess it's the same as journalism,' he says. 'I have a deadline and I just get on and write; the place, the location, the landscape are for me incidental and almost irrelevant. I have never had a problem with inspiration. I don't get writer's block. I guess it's years spent in the commercial industry: you had to produce to order and to time so you just get on with it and write. But this is home, this is where I grew up and this is where I want to be now.'

The creator of *Adiemus* attentively passes biscuits and cakes around to everyone and settles into his garden seat.

'Gower people are a breed apart. There is a particular kind of person who lives here, or at least there was. We are almost an island on Gower, a community living on a long peninsula, nearly surrounded on all sides by the sea.

'I used to come and play near here, forty years ago; we'd walk though these fields on the way to the beach. We'd call in at Mrs America's on our way home.'

'Who was Mrs America?' I ask.

'We called her Mrs America because her cousin had been to America,' and with crumbs flying he starts giggling, quaking at the memory, his laugh too infectious now for any straight faces.

'We were a tightly-knit community where everyone knew everyone. Even today, it's not the easiest place to get to, but in those days this place was pretty remote and cut off from the world.'

David Williams

Karl Jenkins conducting 'The Armed Man: A Mass for Peace' at the National Eisteddfod in Swansea, August 2006; Music at the Mill House

First surfing lesson

You never know what to expect when you meet famous people; sometimes their fame makes them aloof and difficult company. But the trappings of greatness don't sit easily on this man. He seems almost embarrassed by his achievements.

Next week he begins working with Dame Kiri Te Kanawa on a new composition, but today we are all captivated by his easy manner.

Outside the house the sun is moving into its matinee performance. From here, we take a slow drive along a short distance crowded with caravans, speed boats on trailers and cars with a full complement of passengers. Next month, the roads will be returned to the farmers and their tractors.

Beyond Burry Green and Higher Muzzard is Llangennith Beach – the surfer's paradise and home for the night. Although I grew up by the sea, I have never tried surfing, preferring that all journeys that have to be taken on water should be accompanied by a boat of some sort. But today, in the last hour before evening, that's all about to change. I'm going to have my first ever surfing lesson.

The VW parked on the burrows and a wetsuit hired, I squeeze into what feels like a new skin one size too small for my body. Kevin and Laura have been surfing this beach all of their lives and have bravely offered to take a break from the water to try to teach me within the space of an hour all they have learnt in a lifetime.

Not being particularly fit or sporty, I didn't like to complain that the half-mile walk to the beach carrying my borrowed surfboard is enough exercise to last me a month.

Our lesson begins on the sand with me lying on the

board gripping it as though we were on a big wave. With Laura leaning over me, trying to improve my hopeless technique, a small crowd of sympathisers gathers to watch as they might when a dead dolphin is found out of water. Convinced that I might learn more quickly in the water, our tutorial moves from the sand to the sea; at least I'll feel less of an idiot making paddling gestures.

Thankfully today there isn't a single wave on the ocean and no chance whatsoever of me trying to stand on a small board while it moves at great speed. Kevin lectures in English at Swansea University and is a patient teacher. He thinks nothing of coming here at dawn every morning before going to work. These people have got their habit bad. But after a half an hour of learning how to pull my body weight through the water to climb on and off the floating board, I can see what the attraction is. Where sailing is a distanced relationship with wind and water, surfing is the closest of marriages. I can see the thrill and the addiction but I'm not sure how long it would take me to be any good at it. The surfers I've watched along the coast are people at the peak of extraordinary physical fitness, capable of swimming against the vast force of the tide; they have groomed muscle and strength where you didn't think it was possible. They are like fish, the supreme athletes of the sea. The simple physical effort of repeatedly clambering onto my board on the water using unfamiliar upper arm muscles leaves me too exhausted to finish answering Kevin's questions. This has been like a boxing match facing a world champ. On the walk back afterwards it feels like my board has doubled its weight in the water and the return journey takes twice as long.

One exhausted novice

For eight hundred years following the Norman conquest, the people of Gower considered themselves a race apart. The geological line separating the fertile limestone areas of the south from the coal measures of the north neatly matched the cultural divide between English and Welsh Gower. Even the language was different, the Gower accent and dialect closer to the west country than to anywhere in Wales. This is hardly surprising since the Normans repopulated the area with settlers from Somerset, and the lime trade between Gower and north Devon continued right up until the late nineteenth century.

Opportunities to hear real Gower speech are rare, for recordings are few, although a CD of folksinger Phil Tanner survives to give a flavour of a forgotten world. Few Gower characters have caught the public imagination as much as Tanner, that 'vitty' man – a 'proper' man – whose distinctive singing style drew the attention of folk enthusiasts across the UK. Originally from a family of weavers from the far west of Gower, Tanner was always ready with a song, performing regularly for the customers of the King's Head at Llangennith. He was a colourful character right up to the end of his life in the nursing home at Penmaen, with unbeatable stamina, a ready wit and a lively repertoire.

Invited to London to record with the BBC in the 1930s, Tanner insisted on taking his dog with him into the recording studio and on stopping outside Buckingham Palace for a rendition of 'God Save the King'. But Gower was his true home and for more than eighty years he contributed generously to its richness. He was an enthusiastic upholder of customs such as the *mabsant* (revels) and the tradition of January wassailing. He took a leading role in the Gower bidding weddings. Dressed smartly, and fortified by beer, he would visit the home of each prospective guest, inviting them to the wedding and 'bidding' or encouraging them to make a suitable donation to the young couple.

When he died, in 1950, it marked the passing of an era, for the relative isolation which gave Gower its distinctiveness was rapidly diminishing, and the cultural mix which produced a character like Phil Tanner could never be recaptured.

Back at Hillend campsite, we surfers are pulling off our wetsuits; there is as much water inside mine as outside.

Far beyond the smart country hotels and bright bed and breakfasts the real hard-core Gower trippers come here to stay. This is minimalist tourism. All that's needed is a field, a small tent and the beach close by. It doesn't get much more basic and any further trappings are simply a distraction from what really matters on a weekend like this: the surf, the sun and the beach. The field sheltering behind the sand dunes is already busy with purple and blue plastic domes in various states of completion. The connoisseurs of canvas will no doubt be somewhat sniffy about a neighbour who'll be kipping in relative comfort behind the front seats of a camper van. Not for me a few hours grappling with tent pegs and guy ropes, oh no.

A few hours ago, this beach was packed. Several thousand sun lovers, oiled and cooking beneath the scorching heat of summer, have vanished. The empty sands at low tide offer the shame-faced evidence of the day: a plastic bag full of filthy nappies discreetly left behind when no one was looking; fast food wrappings and bottled-water containers; empty cans of lager squeezed into an hourglass of forgetfulness. My heart always leaps when I walk onto a beach at evening. It is the place for contemplation and the soul's confession. It is the hour of compline, the time to witness nature's timeless beauty and, sadly, also man's tragic vandalism of our inheritance. It is the moment when my heart soars at all that is wonderful on earth and then breaks at our disdain for the beauty that surrounds us. The older I get, the more I come to loathe those who leave

Splashing till the sun goes down

Llangennith barbecue

a trail of filth in their wake. Those who left their mark here today I hold in the same contempt as vandals and thieves. They have desecrated the high altar at evening and besmirched a thing of great beauty.

The sand is cold now and the shadows are creeping longer behind the dunes, with the sun's ball of fire fast setting into the sea. We gather stones and dry wood. Some of the day's rubbish will be burnt in our fire on the beach. After a day of marvelling at this coast, it would be strange to turn our backs on it for dinner in a pub, so, humping cool-boxes of steak and sausages, bread rolls, wine and beer, we will spend the evening amidst the smoke of our bonfire, watching the waves cover our footsteps on the shore. This is nature's Grand Finale before darkness falls.

There is something quite wonderful about sitting cross-legged on one of the most beautiful beaches in the world, eating a steak baguette (that is perhaps a little too well done), washed down with a beer. We watch branches burning in the fire and listen to the ceaseless roll of the sea. And when we leave, you'll never know we've been there.

On the other side of the dunes the campsite looks like a shanty town of small homes, gentle lamps lighting shadows, residents preparing for bed. We can smell the cooking – meat and onions – before we see the evidence: pans and stoves and full-bellied adults, relaxed and ready for the night.

Too full of booze we try to pass quietly beside the rows of tents and cars, exaggeratedly shushing each other, but few here are asleep or even weary. A couple of small children giggle in their parents' annexe. Further along an attentive young couple enjoy a nightcap before what looks like their first night away.

The VW doesn't do anything quietly, and both my fumbling with the keys and then closing the sliding door seems to echo in the quietening yellow field. Just to be on the safe side, I sit in the driver's seat before getting ready for bed and push the gearlever into first to make sure we don't roll down the slope in the night. The worn plastic bakelite gear knob comes off in my hand with a metallic ting that means it has sheared off its base rather than worked loose. It's too dark to repair now; I pull the small curtains across their wires and fall heavily on the bed, lying as still as possible, hoping that I won't break anything else in Adam's shrine. Then almost straight away, the deep slumber brought on by a day in the sun and sea carries me off to a sleep that is too deep for dreams.

Camping by the sea

Aled Hughes

At Burry Holms

THE TITTY BELL
(a Gower legend)

In Arthur's time a babe forlorn
   before the mighty king was laid,
in sin conceived, in sorrow born,
   his twisted limbs for all displayed.

'The baby's fate let God decide!'
   the king decreed. A wicker boat
was launched upon the Burry tide –
   the tiny child was set afloat.

A wicked storm the rocks did pound
   and to the Worm the cradle blew
where gulls the helpless infant found
   and bore him to a lodging new.

And there above the waters' swell,
   (a nest of feathers for his bed)
the angels brought a great brass bell
   and from that breast the baby fed.

In time the child a saint became
   (a chapel marks his hermit's cell)
and far and wide did spread the fame
   of Cenydd and the titty bell.

ANON

ACKNOWLEDGEMENTS

A project like this filmed over so many months wouldn't be possible without the co-operation of the people who live in the towns and villages we visited and to them my thanks for their patience and good humour. At Aspect Television our crew on the road and back at base were: Rob Finighan, Kate Jordan, Simon Kmiec, Lisa Roberts, Richard Longstaff, Ann Summerhayes and Dafydd Parry. My thanks to Clare Hudson and Martyn Ingram at the BBC for their continuing support for the travel documentaries we've made over the last five years. I must also say a word of thanks to my editors Gail Morris Jones on *Wales Today* and Sali Collins at Radio Wales who have turned a blind eye to yet another summer of regular absences.

Martin Cavaney's splendid photography has been a joy. My thanks to the other talented photographers listed on page 4; to the Gower Society for permission to use their photograph of Phil Tanner; to Viv Sayer and Dyfed Elis-Gruffydd for invaluable factual information. Any errors which remain in the text are my own. Finally Mairwen Prys Jones and the staff at Gomer Press have made the experience of writing the book and seeing it take shape entertaining and amusing – and for that much thanks.

In order to follow the trails of notable writers, extracts were taken from the following publications: *Kilvert, the Victorian,* ed. David Lockwood (Seren 2002); *Letters to his Wife,* Thomas Carlyle (Gollancz 1953); *Madly in All Directions,* Wynford Vaughan-Thomas (Longmans Green 1967); *Twentieth Century Welsh Poems,* Joseph P. Clancy (Gomer 1982); *A Welsh Country Diary,* William Condry (Gomer 1993); *Wild Wales,* George Borrow (Gomer 1995, first published 1862).